*Ki and the Way of
the Martial Arts*

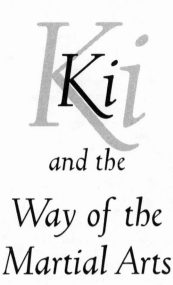

Ki

and the

Way of the Martial Arts

Kenji Tokitsu

Translated by
Sherab Chödzin Kohn

SHAMBHALA

Boston & London

2003

Shambhala Publications, Inc.
Horticultural Hall
300 Massachusetts Avenue
Boston, Massachusetts 02115
www.shambhala.com

Previously published as *Budô: Le Ki et Le Sens Du Combat*
©2000 by Éditions DésIris–Méolans-Revel, France
English translation ©2002 by Shambhala Publications, Inc.

9 8 7 6 5 4 3 2 1

First Shambhala Edition
Printed in the United States of America

♾ This edition is printed on acid-free paper that meets the American
National Standards Institute z39.48 Standard.
Distributed in the United States by Random House, Inc., and in Canada
by Random House of Canada Ltd

Interior Design and Composition: Greta D. Sibley & Associates

Library of Congress Cataloging-in-Publication Data
Tokitsu, Kenji, 1947–
[Budō English]
Ki and the way of the martial arts / Kenji Tokitsu; translated by Sherab
Chödzin Kohn.
p. cm.
ISBN 1-57062-998-6 (Paperback)
1. Martial arts—Japan. 2. Qi (Chinese philosophy) I. Title.
GV1100.77 .T6413 2003
796.8—dc21
2002152898

Contents

Preface

A knife is made to cut. In the same way, the original purpose of the technique of the martial arts was to overcome another person by injuring or killing him. Whatever other goals or justifications have been articulated over time, the technique of the martial arts was developed so that men could fight with other men.

In our society, combat is often cloaked in the forms of disciplines having educational or utilitarian goals. If we compare combat technique to the blade of a sword, depending on the context in which the discipline will be used, this blade must take on a variety of protective coverings to blunt the cutting quality of its edge. For military or policing applications, the blade need only be covered with a thin cloth, but for sports or physical education purposes, the blade has to be carefully placed in a variety of sheathes, which are sometimes decorated with national flags or colors that correspond to various social values.

At present, the relationship between the blade and its protective coverings is problematic, since nowadays anyone can learn the technique of combat through any of a variety of disciplines. We find combat techniques being used in street brawls and in the various kinds of aggressive activities that take place in urban environments. Combat technique has a definite place in the contemporary manifestations of violence. Athletic trainers have made use of combat techniques in educational contexts and have obtained positive results. They have succeeded in channeling the violence of young people into a discipline, and on this account they consider training in combat technique educational. Naturally, their local communities approve of this. Nonetheless, it seems to me that that which limits antisocial or criminal use of combat technique, the equivalent of the sheath, is quite fragile so long as this restraint remains a matter of individual responsibility alone. An individual who knows how to use dangerous techniques is at the same time a moral being. A balance is achieved in the juxtaposition of dangerous techniques and the moral sense. We are all caught up in a network of varying pressures, and certain persons and groups have an interest in allowing violence and aggression to erupt. To what extent can we place our confidence in the individual morality of people today?

Society accepts programs that teach and develop techniques intended to overpower others physically, techniques intended to kill. How can we justify this within the framework of physical education? This reality is masked by giving such programs the trappings of a sport and providing the excuse of letting off steam. "Combat exercises make me feel good, they are good for my health. . . ." How these techniques are applied remains a matter of individual responsibility. In the West, combat training is regarded as a technique and therefore as a means to an end. As a result, it does not include morality; the morality involved is considered an add-on.

A particular quality of Japanese *budo*, which can doubtless also be found in other traditions, is that it includes a moral sense within its technical character.

The point is that in order to guarantee the result, the morality or the ethics of the martial arts must derive directly from the body and from practical technique. It cannot be something imposed externally. Since we are dealing with a situation in which budo is confused with combat activities in general, I think it is useful, indeed necessary, to provide a precise description of the cultural significance of budo and the perspective it offers to people who become interested in it. Budo presents a dimension of human activity that might be interesting for people who think of the practice of the martial arts as something quite alien to them. Seeing the budo aspect might even serve to attract them to this practice. Budo is a particular physical practice that leads without fail to spiritual development. In fact, if people begin budo as a physical practice, their path will guide them progressively toward a psychological dimension, and they will encounter a practice in which the body and the mind form a unity. However, the possibility of this is greatly reduced today by the confusion that exists between budo and many kinds of violent activities. The purpose of the present work is to make clear to the reader the approach and the particular factors through which combat can be practiced as budo so that it becomes a means for the cultivation of the entire human being.

The term "budo" has become almost synonymous with "a martial art of Japanese origin." It is one of many terms connected with the activity of combat that people use more or less interchangeably, without questioning their meaning. Quite a number of people talk about "practicing budo," which has the virtue of imparting a touch of elegance to the brutality of combat. But the real study of budo is actually very narrow. One of the main reasons is that the Oriental martial arts have not been accorded an appropriate position in the West. They have been relegated to the fringes of the sports world, where competition is the most important element. In addition to this, the martial arts have been linked with violence and everything connected with it. They have been put to use in a variety of applications: in shows, as a form of entertainment, in various forms of self-defense—military combat or combat in the context of police work—and also in street fighting. The utilitarian aspect takes precedence in the West, and study of the cultural qualities of the martial arts seems to be largely overlooked.

Noh theater, the tea ceremony, haiku, Bunraku, Kabuki, and other such disciplines were developed in a society dominated by the sword. This implies a conception of life and death that is different from the one prevailing in our times. The sensibility of these cultural endeavors was shaped by people living in this time in which the sword played a decisive role. The deep meaning of the Japanese martial arts is inseparable from this cultural context. In Japan, the warrior culture lives on today in the manifest form of the martial arts, and in a more general way, it underlies all the behavior of the Japanese people.

In spite of this, the practice of budo is not as evident for contemporary Japanese people as one might think. Since the modernization of Japan, the appearance of the Japanese city has changed, and the Japanese way of life (even the way Japanese people move) has been profoundly shaken and transformed in a number of ways. What remains of the traditional culture is now deeply buried beneath social appearances. For example, until the beginning of the Meiji period, the Japanese walked differently.

Permitting ourselves to caricature things slightly, we can say that the following typical styles were current at the end of Edo period. A warrior walked holding his hand near his sword, which was stuck in his sash, and directed his movements from the center of gravity of his belly. A merchant walked with small steps, with his body leaning forward and his hands resting on top of his apron. An artisan walked without swinging his body or his tools and kept his knees supple. A farmer walked with his body leaning forward and his hands on the load he was carrying on his shoulders. The ethic of the feudal social order reinforced these physical patterns and ended up turning them into fixed elements of identity.

So the Japanese of the feudal period did not walk as Japanese people do today, with their arms swinging. This style of walking was introduced by Westerners, and the Japanese way of walking changed. For from the time of the restoration of 1868, Japan adopted the Western educational system in the domain of intellectual knowledge as well as in that of physical education. The power of modern Japan was based on this new educational system, which quickly spread throughout the country. In tandem with a rapid reduction in the illiteracy rate, the modern style of physical education was imposed with the idea of training soldiers according to the Western model. This profoundly altered the physical comportment of the Japanese.

The Japanese have continued to practice the traditional martial arts, but the physical movements used in these arts have ceased to be, as they originally were, extensions of the gestures of everyday life, because the pattern of physical behavior has changed. The objectives of the martial arts were also transformed as these disciplines were adapted to the new system of values. In a certain sense, the Japanese of today practice the traditional martial arts with a body trained to emulate a corpus of everyday gestures that has been in the process of disappearing for more than a century. Inevitably, this has led to a change in the quality and character of these arts.

I want to stress this first point, because it is often overlooked. When Westerners study the traditional Japanese martial arts as they are transmitted today, they are unaware of the extent to which these martial arts have been influenced by their own culture.

Ki

and the

Way of the
Martial Arts

Shinjo tetsu seki, "Mind like iron ore,"
by the monk Kawashima

I

What Is Budo?

Contrary to an idea that is widespread in martial arts circles, budo is not a direct replica of the martial arts as practiced by the warriors of the past. It is a modern conception that has as its aim the training of the human being as a whole, both intellectually and physically, making use of the traditional disciplines of combat. As we have seen, it is a traditional practice done with modern physical behavior patterns, which it calls into question.

In Japan, the term "budo" is used in a rather confused way. It is a general term that covers all the martial disciplines. At the same time, it cannot be said with regard to any discipline that a beginner is practicing budo, because that implies a certain way of practicing. When people talk about the spirit of practicing kendo, judo, or karate, they often give an additional qualification, linked by the word *as*. For example, kendo (judo, karate) as a competitive sport or kendo (judo, karate) as budo.

"Budo" evokes images of seriousness, of severity, of ritual, of respect for the ancients and the master, of silent meditation, and so on. So budo gives the impression of a conservative practice and an austere attitude. The word "dojo" evokes the serenity of a solemn space with a polished wooden floor. These images contrast with those of a sport that takes place in a brightly lit gymnasium or outdoors. Indeed, as soon as we speak of sports, the image is freer and in some way more sunlit.

In Japan, when people talk about budo in regard to karate, it sometimes refers to a hard and violent practice with competitions in which fighting to the KO is not avoided; or it sometimes refers to an austere practice that distances itself from competitions and favors real combat, in which blood and injuries are not avoided. Some people associate it with ascetic training in the mountains. Violent confrontation is one of its characteristics.

In other disciplines such as archery (*kyudo*), stress is placed on the spiritual aspect and on harmony in the ceremonial aspect of the practice—to the point where the idea of combat is excluded.

Thus in Japan a tendency exists to define budo in accordance with its hard and austere aspect. But this definition is more emotional than theoretical and cannot take us very far. As far as severity and high risk are concerned, there are disciplines in the realm of sport, such as mountain climbing or sailboat racing where, in their extreme form, the risks are much greater. Therefore it is imprecise to define budo in terms of austerity and severity or in terms of a spirit of asceticism.

What is budo then? The very notion of budo implies the need to reflect on the technical practice of the martial arts, *bu*, in connection with notion of "way," *do*. The term dates from the Edo period and means "the way of the warrior." After the Meiji period, its meaning shifted to designate the martial way in a society that was being transformed through importation of Western models. At present, it is a very ambiguous term.

My intention is to study the concept of budo as it is used to refer to the practice of our contemporaries.

In Japan today, modernity is highly prized, and the moment anyone speaks of a "way," *do*, some people are immediately put off. It is nevertheless my opinion that this notion remains a presence in contemporary Japanese culture. As it is manifested in budo, the way is neither archaic nor mystical. Its practice is not limited to Asians but has been offered very openly as a way of seeking a certain form of perfection that any person can develop on the basis of physical exercises. It seems to me that the manner in which certain mountain climbers and sailing enthusiasts take their discipline to the extreme point by putting their very lives on the line is close to the idea of "way," because they are seeking by means of very demanding physical techniques to confer meaning on their lives through experiences in which they confront death.

Using an analysis of the practice of the martial arts as the basis, I would like to describe the principal characteristics of the Japanese conception of the way. It is the entirety of one's life, from the moment of birth to the moment of death, that constitutes the way. It includes uphill passages and downhill passages. Every person treads this way, but the way does not impose itself on one's consciousness, and it is easy to become scattered with the passage of time. From the moment that we speak of the way, there is the sense of a direction or a goal. But as long as this sense is not experienced as a practice, the chances are that budo will remain an abstraction, even if a person has a historical and cultural knowledge of it.

When, during this span of time that is our life, we associate with the practice of the martial arts a sense of striving to better oneself, that is, to improve oneself as a totality, the idea of budo is born, regardless of what culture this idea originates in.

The idea of self-improvement is presented in all cultures. Nevertheless, what the Japanese meant by it seems to me very different from what Westerners understand by it. The difference in these conceptions is masked by the notion of progress and does not make its appearance right away. If Westerners wish to practice budo in a complete manner, one of the most important problems they face, it seems to me, is putting into practice the idea of the way. An analysis of the problems encountered in the process of transmitting the practice of budo in a culture other than the Japanese will permit us to attain a better understanding of the complexity of this notion.

2

The Transmission of Budo
by the Japanese

*L*et us begin with the difficulties or the explicit and implicit problems that Japanese masters of the martial arts encounter in attempting to transmit budo to foreigners who want to develop a martial arts practice.

For the Japanese masters, one of the primary difficulties is communicating physical techniques as linked with spiritual aspects. For if they really wish to be understood, they will be forced to adopt a relative conception of life so as to accommodate the view of Westerners, which will lead them, in a sense, to call into question their own view of the world. This is not an easy thing.

To make progress in the practice of budo, concentration, will, conviction, and even an immovable spirit are required in order to persevere through years of training. The will needed for long, hard periods of training is not necessarily compatible with an attempt at in-depth theoretical and logical reflection. The majority of masters draw the energy that is needed to nourish the practice of budo from the sensation of seeking perfection, even when they do not do so consciously.

For masters of the generation that lived through the Second World War, this sensation derives from an approach that aims at reaching the state of perfection represented by a syncretistic fusion of the image of Buddha and the image of the Shinto gods. This image of perfection is a value that is profoundly present in Japanese society. It contains an intuition of the oneness of the human world and the whole universe. This tendency toward universalism is very general in budo circles. Moreover, the steadfastness and the intense effort demanded by budo tend to reinforce the vision of the universality of the value of life as led upon the way—because plurality can lead to a loss of direction, *mayoi*. Budo makes it possible to forge the strength to go directly toward the goal, even, sometimes, at the expense of critical thought.

The idea of universal truth involves a tendency toward simplification and toward justifications that could lead to totalitarianism. It is also the basis for all the sects. Let us not forget that it was one of the justifications for the ideology of world domination during the Second World War. It is not merely by chance that, during the wars, budo was easily blended with a nationalism that excluded all values other than those of imperial Japan. This universalism can also express itself in terms of generosity—for example, when foreign students are received in a dojo in Japan—to the degree that the point of view of the Japanese masters is not challenged or shaken. But then this attitude derives principally from an illusion of understanding that is made possible by the inability to communicate adequately through language. I have seen the same pattern repeat itself many times: a master says that his Western followers understand the spirit of budo better than his Japanese students do. When a problem appears, he says, "Foreigners are, after all, foreigners; they will never understand budo." When misunderstandings come out into the open, these same masters can seem egocentric, incomprehensible, or hermetic to their Western students. I believe that some Western students have had this kind of experience.

It must be recognized that few Japanese masters are inclined to acquire an understanding of systems of thought other than the Japanese, especially in relation to the practice of budo. But their attitude also reflects the absence of personal openness of someone who is fully committed to studying and understanding something, an approach that is not natural to the Japanese culture. For the majority of older masters, budo is unique, and, as a result, the communication of budo can only be a one-way thing: from the master to the disciples and from the Japanese to the foreigners. It is unthinkable to them that the concept of budo could be reexamined and modified or clarified through cultural contact with foreigners. However, I think it is time to reexamine and clarify the concept of budo, because the practice of budo has now become worldwide, and it seems to me that this situation is becoming more and more firmly established.

If Japanese masters are not capable of communicating budo correctly to the outside world, budo outside Japan runs the risk of taking on an unrecognizable face and losing the specific character that makes it what it is. The responsibility of the Japanese masters, especially in the case of kendo, is all the greater because masters of a high level are incomparably more numerous in Japan than in other countries. Their responsibility is multifaceted and heavy, because, as I see it, kendo is at present the only discipline in which the idea of budo as elaborated through the practice of combat is preserved in its full sense. As for the other budo disciplines, by contrast, some have become mixed up with combat sports and others are confined to the nearly exclusive practice of *kata* (forms), which—mistakenly—makes them seem like folkloric practices. It must also be recognized that today the integrity of kendo is threatened to the point where its very foundation has become fragile.

In this situation, the responsibility of the Japanese masters and students is first and foremost to preserve a cultural heritage—the heritage of kendo and budo—and develop it further and, second, to communicate it and transmit it to others. Using the example of the kendo tradition as a basis, masters of other disciplines must learn the elements that their disciplines are lacking so as to give them the genuine qualities of budo. I would say that a discipline like karate possesses the potential to go further than present-day kendo in the realm of budo because the practical model of karate is more adapted to modernity, whereas no one can fail to see the disparity between kendo and modernity. Nonetheless, the budo consciousness of the karate practitioner is far behind that of the kendo practitioner.

In reality today, self-examination concerning their quality of budo is in order for practitioners of all the traditional Japanese martial arts disciplines. In responding to this questioning, it is necessary to have a broad vision of the world of budo. Broad vision is needed in order to analyze the current situation of Japan and other countries and to develop a theory and method for the communication of budo that is capable of responding to this situation fully. For these reasons, I think that evolution and progress on the part of Japanese masters and students is essential.

These positive and negative factors seem to me to reflect problems that are fundamental in intercultural communication.

As a matter of fact, a current theme of discussion in Japan is the possibility of practicing budo as a means of cultivating the whole human being and of propagating the various budo disciplines on a global scale. From my point of view, such an attempt makes sense only if we discover another way of grasping the essence of budo that dissociates it from the Japanese cosmogony. It is this dimension of Japanese budo that I am dedicated to defining. Only that dimension will make it possible for me to convey within Western culture what the essence of budo is. To go a little further, in my opinion there is not one single budo, but rather there are multiple possibilities for the practice and appreciation of budo.

In this situation, I will go so far as to say that the majority of Japanese masters, especially the older ones, have very little awareness of the multiplicity of visions of life with which budo is confronted today, mainly because of their education and also because of language barriers and their lack of experience in communicating with foreigners.

3

The Problem of Budo for Foreign Practitioners

What are the problems most frequently encountered by foreign students, particularly Westerners?

The way, for the Japanese, is related to the whole of one's lifetime. The notion of budo involves striving for the betterment of oneself, that is to say, the betterment of one's being in its totality, by means of the practice of martial arts. This expression is understandable for Westerners, but they do not attach the same meaning to it as the Japanese do.

The way to elevate the quality of being human through the practice of budo is derived in Japan, as we have seen, from Buddhist and Shinto ideas. People are capable of attaining the Buddha state, a divine state, and are capable of becoming one with the god of a particular shrine. We can cite, for example, the Hayashisaki-Jinja shrine, where the founder of the Iai school, Hayashizaki Jinsuke-Shigenobu, is venerated as the equal of a god. A large number of shrines exist where a person is worshiped as a god. This notion presupposes that people are capable, through their efforts, of arriving at a state of perfection during their lives. All people have the potential, by raising their human worth, of changing the quality of their being and attaining a level of merit that is inseparable from a form of the absolute. This vision is manifestly different from that of the Christian culture, where the distance between humans and God is insurmountable.

Philosophical discussion and ethics in the Japanese martial arts or budo are based fundamentally on the Buddhist and Shinto conception of the world and a universe in which there is no absolute because nothing exists that is relative. The universe is not founded on the concept of God/Absolute. I know several Japanese martial arts masters who are Christians. Though their faith may be Christian, that does not prevent them from having a sense of the universal energy in the Shinto and Buddhist way.

Budo rests on this conception of the world and this form of sensibility, and within that, the idea of training oneself, cultivating oneself, is central. To develop this idea in the context of other cultures would be, in a certain way, to extend the generosity of the Buddhist logic of giving birth to accomplishment by effacing oneself. Every person is considered capable of the aspiration of seeking perfection by traveling the way. In budo, this quest is pursued through intensive training in physical techniques.

Through this process, the practice of budo, in a sense, leads Western students, like Japanese masters, to doubt and question their way of being. For Westerners this is not a question of adopting what we might call Japanese-ism. Some Westerners seem to live in a more Japanese way than the Japanese. I think that dropping one's own identity or making it ambiguous does not help; quite the contrary, the approach of budo leads to a strengthening of identity by causing one to live intensely in the here and now every moment. Practicing budo outside Japan means that practitioners have to develop their own identity without relying on Japanese models.

Certain Western experts define budo in another way; they note the common characteristics of the various martial arts disciplines. In this way they end up with a catalog that has no structure. Their approach fails to take into consideration the specific quality of budo, which abides in the notion of training or cultivating the human being rather than in the particularities of the movements employed in the various disciplines.

Jisei Budo, "Form the budo through which one forms oneself,"
by Misako Tokitsu

自成武道

4

A Key to Budo

The idea of the way appears spontaneously when the striving toward personal fruition is associated with the progressive practice of martial arts over time. In other words, as long as this sense of striving does not appear, the practice cannot contain the idea of the way, and, as a result, it will not be budo.

In the narrow sense of the term, budo does not designate any particular martial arts discipline, but rather the quality and the content of the manner in which one practices a discipline. So it is not because you seriously practice kendo, aikido, karate-do, the art of the staff (*jodo*), archery (kyudo)—in short, any of the various disciplines that have the suffix *do*—that you practice budo. It is when your practice of the physical discipline spontaneously contains this striving toward the cultivation of yourself as a whole person, the striving that is proper to the way, that it becomes budo. Your practice will then begin, through the technique, to become inseparable from seeking meaning in life. I pointedly say "through the technique," because the meaning of life can be associated with any other activity. In budo, the quest for quality in the technique is directly connected with the quest for meaning in life.

Thus budo does not constitute a particular genre among the disciplines of combat, but rather the manner in which you engage in a discipline of the art of combat in seeking efficacy.

Therefore it is appropriate to think of budo in two senses: as a type of discipline and as a subjective relationship. For example, as soon as you start practicing kendo, aikido, or karate by joining an association or a dojo, you are practicing one of the disciplines of budo. But the content of your practice will remain merely that of a combat sport of Oriental origin as long as you fail to discover in your way of applying it a subjective sense of training and cultivating yourself, or as long as there is no fusion of the process of bettering your technique and the process of bettering your whole being.

I find it interesting to cite a passage from a letter I received at the beginning of 1999 from a master of kendo, a man seventy-seven years of age, whom I respect a great deal and consider one of my teachers on the way of budo. I want to present this passage because it perfectly illustrates this process and the difficulties it entails. The words and phrases of this passage evoke a kind of intuition; they are personal and will not be clear to everyone, because they are not based on the usual kind of reasoning, but they take on meaning for a person who is practicing budo.

At present, I am directing the midwinter training, *kangeiko*, from 5:30 to 7:00 A.M. The light of the stars is that of *ki*, the movement of the clouds is that of ki, and the sun emanates the ki that burns, which is the ki of taking initiative, *sen*. The ki of the cosmos, more distant than the sun, is the ki of anticipated initiative, *sen-sen*. I continue in my training, using my precious time to strengthen myself through ki while strengthening and nourishing it, in order to get closer to the universal truth. I make efforts to reach the stage of going beyond life and death, in order to let my being fuse with the universe. This is the most peaceful moment for me to communicate silently with the universe. This is the return to the self and the return to emptiness. I train myself by holding the bamboo sword, the *shinai*, as the sword with which I try to bring about the fusion of technique and understanding.

For me this text is perfectly clear, and I perceive it through the concrete sensations of the living experience of budo that it evokes in me. In reading this text, a Japanese, even if he does not practice budo, fills in and completes that which is left vague—for the ambiguous space of these sentences is filled by the content of the notion of ki, a word that evokes physical sensations. Translated into English, each word takes on a precise connotation, and this mode of speech does not leave empty space anymore. The expression is very personal and is understood in this way in Japanese. Translated into English, it takes on a universal sense that it did not have in its original language.

The striving toward the cultivation of self in the sense in which I have spoken of it does not appear here in an abstract way but in a way that is based on concrete bodily sensation. This is a bodily sensation that any human being can understand, regardless of cultural origin. In other words, this bodily sensation is the key that allows anyone to practice budo fully and completely, going beyond cultural obstacles.

What does this bodily sensation consist of? In Japanese it is expressed by the idea of ki. We have just seen an example of this.

How can you be sure that your martial arts practice is becoming budo and that you are not creating an illusion? There is an element that serves to indicate this, that makes budo budo and at the same time supports you in your progress. This is ki. In this sense, ki is the key to the practice of budo. We are speaking here of an inner certainty, which is extremely difficult to explain in words but is communicable physically. That is why, after having clarified the Japanese notion of ki, we shall examine how it is practiced in relation to different situations, in order to fully grasp this unique notion that simultaneously engages the body and the mind.

5

Ki in Japanese Culture

In the Japanese language, a great number of expressions contain the word "ki," and others presuppose it. I had to deal with this situation when I was translating the text of Miyamoto Musashi's *Writings on the Five Elements* for my book *Miyamoto Musashi.**

In this text, Musashi uses the word *kokoro* a great number of times. This word is usually translated as "mind," but it cannot be translated by a single word. Depending on the context, kokoro may be translated as "mind, feeling, sensation, sense, thought, idea, meaning, essence, heart, center, core," and so on.

Nevertheless, even after using these various words to translate kokoro, there remains a sense of incompleteness in the translation. I spent a long time trying to figure out why this was so before I understood that Musashi, in using words, was assuming as a basis a sensation that the Japanese of the period, especially practitioners of the martial arts, were familiar with and shared. He was, in a way, investing this medium of expression with all his actual lived experience. (I

---

*Kenji Tokitsu, *Miyamoto Musashi* (Éditions DésIris, 1998).

am using the word "medium" here in the sense of a medium or binder for pigments, for example, oil.) That is why, as long as we have not grasped the nature of this medium, Musashi's expressions will remain incomplete—in a sense, as though seen with only one eye. They will remain ambiguous. If we are aware of the implicit presence of this medium, his expressions will become substantial. What is the medium? Here again, we are talking about ki.

In fact, once I had read his text and completed it by holding in mind the underlying feeling of ki, its meaning became much clearer. But how do we make this unspoken element come across in the English language? This is the fundamental problem in the translation of Japanese texts, particularly the ancient ones.

It is also necessary to understand that the significance of writing was different for the Japanese of Musashi's time. For example, in the written certificate of transmission we often find the words "If it should happen that I betray this trust, I should be punished by such and such gods" used by both the master who is granting the certificate and the disciple who is receiving it. Thus at the end of the certificate of transmission written by Kamiizumi Nobutsuna for Yagyu Sekishusai, we find the following sentence: "If it should happen that I betray that which I have just written, I should be punished by Marishiten, Hachiman Daibosatsu, Tenman Tenjin, Kasuga Daimyojin, and Atagoyama."

Citing the names of several gods in this way was a testament to the most serious of commitments. Writing the name of a god indicated a commitment on the level of life and death. The Japanese of the period were pervaded by a sense of the presence of the divine in nature. This atmosphere aroused an awareness of the sensation of ki. Not so long ago, the Japanese people still lived with a sense of the importance of that which is not visible. In my memories of my childhood in Japan, this kind of sensation is present.

Through the sensation of ki, the Japanese seem to have grasped the sense of natural phenomena without trying to explain them. They did not exclude vague sensations from the domain of speech. I think this is one of the reasons that we find a great many onomatopoeic words in the Japanese language. When they needed to verbalize the intermediating element, the medium that corresponded to certain vague sensations or feelings, the Japanese used the word "ki." As a result, the sensation of ki seems to be situated on a deeper and more archaic level than sensations that became objects of knowledge.

One of the peculiarities of Japanese culture and society seems to me to be the fact that the Japanese continued to give an important place to this type of perception even as they went on to develop a modern logic.

6

The Japanese Conception of Ki

I believe that the bodily sensation of ki is commonly present in human experience but that the form taken by the interpretation of this sensation varies from culture to culture. For example, the logical aspect is much more developed in Western languages than in the Japanese language. In Western languages, there does not exist—and this is one of the major difficulties for translation—a word equivalent to ki. In Japanese this term covers various sensations and impressions that are mysterious, vague, and intangible, that touch upon something in the deepest part of our being, something that is connected with a level of insight that is probably archaic or repressed.

This difficult-to-define body of impressions is present in the experience of the everyday life, the literature, and the arts of Japan. When it is necessary to name it, people call it ki.

The exclusion of these sensations and impressions from the explicit terminology of Western languages seems to me to be a corollary of the logical character of these languages. Rational thought probably developed through the repression of this sensibility. Space is pervaded by different energies, and we know that this space exists without being able to define its content. Daily we use television sets, radios, and portable telephones that use electromagnetic waves that are neither visible or tangible without special equipment. It was only in relatively recent times that science was able to demonstrate the existence of these waves. However, when it comes to ki, it is not rare for people who consider themselves rational to reject the idea a priori, because ki is not tangible and doubtless more profoundly because it is connected with subjective experience. The fact is that ki is not an abstract conception; it is a conception that arises out of listening to the bodily sensations through which one perceives one's environment and also, at the same time, the manner in which one is situated within it.

Ki is felt by means of the body and is given a more or less defined representation depending on the culture in question. The sensation of ki is intensified when speculative self-consciousness is pushed into the background. This happens to varying degrees depending on how much people are willing to let go of their ego in deferring to what surrounds them. If ego is reinforced, the sensation of ki diminishes. In a certain way, the state of mind of heightened ki awareness runs counter to the Cartesian process. In being attentive to the sensation of ki, you dissolve into your surroundings through the effacement of the central sensation of your own existence. This attitude is at the root of the different techniques for strengthening ki.

These techniques, which were religious in origin, have also long been used for therapeutic purposes. Today in Japan and China, methods of therapy are being developed in which such techniques are separated from their mystical origins and applied in tandem with medical means for healing by stimulating ki.

In Japanese, ki is not defined by clarifying its characteristics; rather the term is used when one feels the presence of something that cannot be clearly grasped. The Japanese language leaves an undefined space in its mode of expression. It seems to me that it is only by means of the body that we can explore this space; in clarifying the role of this space, we can advance in the area of physical technique.

The same ideogram is pronounced *qi* in Chinese and *ki* in Japanese. Even though the meaning is similar for the most part, there are certain differences between the Japanese idea of ki and the Chinese idea of qi. In both countries, disciplines intended to develop the capacity for qi or ki have existed for a long time. They have been propagated since the 1970s under the name *qigong* in Chinese and *kiko* in Japanese. In the present work, I shall limit myself to attempting to shed light on the Japanese conception of ki as it applies to the domain of the martial arts.

According to Japanese thought, ki is an entity that enables life and the existence of things in the universe. It is thus more than "vital energy," as it is usually translated. Ki exists in things that appear to us to be devoid of organic life, such as stones, and also in natural phenomena like wind or rain. Ki also resides in mountains, in the sea, and so on. Seen in this way, ki appears as an extension of primitive animist thought. Nonetheless, today when civilization is confronted with a different set of problems, including the destruction of natural environments, this line of thought, rejected for a time as archaic, is now raising new questions.

A number of trends exist today that are attempting to recover qualities of the human being that are supposed to have been lost in the course of "progress." There is no doubt that the sharpness of our senses of hearing, smell, touch, and sight, which played a vital role in the distant past, has been dulled, as our senses have been supplanted by material devices. This has caused questions to be raised about other perceptive capacities that modern humans might have lost and has brought about interest in various methods for achieving well-being. Research in this area has brought to light buried perceptive capacities of the body and has led to the discovery of a new level of perception, which scientific advances have made accessible. Many attempts have been made to find scientific explanations for the mysteries hidden in the human being. Freud's concept of libido touches upon this profound something-or-other in human nature, and I believe it coincides partially with the idea of ki.

In the perspective that developed in Japan, studying and developing ki in the practice of budo or kiko consists on the whole of becoming sensitive to the ki in one's own body, then to the external phenomenon of ki, and finally to the ki of the universe. This implies being permeable to the ki of the universe and feeling that one's body is part of the universe filled with ki.

At the stage where the sensation of ki is sufficiently developed, the ki of the body is in harmony with the ki of the universe. The various methods of kiko are methods through which people seek to become permeable to the reality of universal ki. The ultimate stage of the practice of kiko is *furen shuten*, in which the body becomes permeable to ki to the highest possible degree. At that point, you have mastery over ki without the slightest intention. You are in free communication with the universal ki; without needing exercises, you live with ki. This is the ultimate stage, the ideal aimed at by those who practice kiko.

The idea of universal ki can be made compatible with Western thought only with difficulty, but I must stress that implicitly or explicitly it is essential to the Japanese conception of ki.

Without reaching the point of furen shuten, when we have sufficiently developed our sensitivity to ki, we become aware that our mental activity is inseparable from that of ki. At this level, we can feel a correlation between words and ki; in connection with words ki is subject to more or less weighty pressures. The fact of naming things, of precisely defining the sense of things or the sense of our actions, inevitably brings about a modulation of our ki, because the contour of ki as it is defined by the words, when the meaning is narrowly circumscribed, eliminates any latent meaning. Clarifying and defining implies eliminating or suppressing the vague and imprecise contours of the latent sense. This way of defining it in words implies a reduction of ki, which is always global, holistic. Thus to name a feeling of love represses the hatred that is contained in it. Buddhism teaches us to confront this conglomerate of feelings without basing distinctions on circumscribed oppositions as in the Western style. Thus "love" can be translated by *ai* and "hate" by *nikushimi(zo)*, but a maxim of Buddhist origin affirms that the two amount to the same thing.

If we constitute ourselves as social beings by means of words, at the same time the cutting-up of things that the words imply eliminates a part of the reality of our lived experience and, as a result, shuts out a significant part of the ki. Thus it is not by chance that the Taoists as well as the Buddhists seek a mental state that is detached from the system of words. They seek to grasp the essence of things without de-limiting and deforming it through words. This is the state of emptiness or nonthought.

Thus the system of words with which we are so deeply impregnated is also one of the obstacles encountered in the practice of ki.

However, we are not at all suggesting trying to regain the state of a primitive human being. We are talking about an effort to recover or reestablish the qualities, the sensitivities, or the faculties that we have lost in the course of the development of our civilization. In a certain way, kiko aims at endowing the civilized being with primitive qualities that we have lost. So it is not a question of attempting to go backward. On the contrary, we are talking about an effort on the part of civilized beings to go beyond the barriers with which they have been confronted and about their doing this by mobilizing their own means to reestablish faculties that are still potentially present.

Words appear, ki is modulated in accordance with their sense, and it is reduced in the process. How can we detach ourselves from words while living with language? This is one of the keys to the methods of kiko. In kiko, we use images, sounds, and movements rather than words in order to increase depth beyond words, in order to lead our being into the world of ki.

7

The Content of Combat in Kendo

*T*o go beyond cultural obstacles and obtain the key to budo, it is necessary to cultivate our sensitivity to the sensation of ki and to allow ourselves to be guided in breadth and in depth by this sensation by means of the physical techniques of combat. Apprenticeship in kendo is exemplary for an exploration of ki through techniques of progressive training.

In kendo, the student learns at the beginning what ki is in a simple way, through the expression *ki ken tai ichi*, which designates the simultaneous integration of ki, the sword, and the body in the technique of striking. Over the years, the practitioner of kendo will learn how important it is to take the offensive in the course of combat. One of the basic methods for arriving at this is *seme*. This complex notion merits an explanation, because, in practice, the level of the practitioner is directly reflected in the quality of the practitioner's seme.

Seme literally means "offense" in the sense of an offense on the mental level and not in the sense of an offensive physical gesture. Nevertheless, seme consists in a movement of attack or the simulation of one. Here a type of opposition between the body and the mind comes into play that is appreciably different from the classic Western opposition between the two. I will call it a Japanese dualism. The mind guides the body, but at a certain moment, the situation can be reversed. Generally speaking, one can reach the mind through the body, and the mind is capable of being strengthened by physical practice. Moreover, if the body, guided by the mind, accomplishes a certain breakthrough, it places itself on the same plane as the mind—at that point one can speak of a fusion of body and mind. On this basis, your body can conquer the mind of another. Practitioners of the martial arts who have gone beyond certain limits, or monks who have practiced certain ascetic physical exercises, attain this fusion, and various methods have been elaborated to accomplish it. In traditional Japanese belief, it is normal to consider that great masters are capable of exerting power over spirits or demons that an ordinary person is incapable of even facing.

This conception has a defining role in the Japanese martial arts. It brings up the idea that in order to conquer physically, it is necessary first to conquer the mind; after that, it is through conquering the body that one can totally conquer the mind. Seme expresses itself in movements, but these are aimed at first striking the mind of your opponent.

In the course of an apprenticeship in kendo, you begin the approach to seme through attitudes or movements that communicate your combativeness to your opponent. Seme involves a lot more than just the feints that are used in fighting. The notion of seme is much more profound than that of the feint. For a feint to succeed, your opponent has to confuse it with a movement of actual attack. The feint is a tactic to make your opponent believe that the false is true. It is aimed at provoking a suitable reaction. In the West, people speak of a successful or unsuccessful feint and in so doing describe only the movement, because the notion of seme does not exist. If the feint succeeds, it is because it has constituted what is called seme in Japanese. The point is, if the feint succeeds, it is because your gesture, as minimal as it may have been, has succeeded in troubling the mind of your opponent. That is why it would be inaccurate to define the process of learning seme by describing movements. The gesture of seme is one that communicates something essential.

At a more advanced level, you try to cause a movement in the mind of your opponent without producing any outward sign. At this stage, you take the offensive mainly through ki. This is called *kizeme*: succeeding in disconcerting your opponent through the ki emanating from your person without any visible gesture. The difference between seme and kizeme resides in the place occupied by movement or gesture. What the two have in common is that they both aim at causing a shift in the mind of your opponent by means of ki—the need to link this with a gesture, a movement, is more or less great depending on your level.

"Causing a shift in the mind of your opponent" means that this act causes in your opponent the movement of an entire accumulation of combat experience, actualizing bodily memories on which anticipation is based. Thus those who have no experience of combat will not react in a technical way in response to seme or kizeme.

Looked at in another way, what you are doing is playing a subtle game inherent in combat, nothing more. What is it about this tactic that could make it an element in the cultivation and training of the whole human being? What makes it possible for you to influence your opponent is not a movement, false or real; it is the fact that you put the weight of your existence into the act. It is only through doing this that your act takes on value at the moment of combat. Seme achieves significance by reflecting the weight of your being. It is through that that you can avoid being troubled by the seme of your adversary. "The weight of your being" here means body and mind. Your body can be troubled even if you think your mind is lucid. Your mind can be troubled even if your body seems stable. Because of this, the game of appearances of seme brings body and mind to bear directly. Because of this, seme constitutes the fundamental framework of budo combat. It is through seme that we can explore the mental domain of budo. This notion was developed in the practice of kendo. But the possibility exists for the other martial arts in which there is striking or blows to integrate seme in order to go beyond the simple level of fighting to win. It is for this reason that I shall undertake an analysis of combat in kendo.

Kendo is a modern discipline of martial arts developed from the art of the sword of Japanese warriors. It is practiced with swords made of laminated bamboo (shinai) and helmets and protective armor. This form was devised at the beginning of the nineteenth century and evolved along with the modernization of Japan. After the Second World War, it underwent a reform that gave it its present form. Like Western fencing, it is a form of combat with precise rules in which two adversaries confront each other. Strikes are limited to the head, the wrists, and the torso, and thrusts with the point to the throat

and chest. Protective padding makes it possible to avoid in-
jury, but the blows can be felt and are painful to a certain extent—enough to create apprehension about being attacked.

During a kendo match, if you concentrate your attention
on the way in which the combatants cross their shinai, you
will see that when the points cross, they make subtle movements, which are sometimes calm, sometimes light and rapid.
This is the combat of points, the implicit combat in which
practitioners of kendo engage to take control of their opponent's central line, or vital line, in order to impose their initiative of attack, to create a situation in which their strike is
sure to land successfully. The most important combat takes
place in this not particularly dynamic-looking exchange. Here
we find the meaning of the famous maxim "Do not win after
having struck, but strike after having won." "After having
won" specifically means after having won in the combat of
points and of seme.

The moment when the two adversaries face each other
is the moment when what I shall analyze as the interplay of
ki begins. The gestures of seme are a means of projecting ki
onto your opponent. If the act of seme influences the attitude
of your opponent, it is because this act touches and causes a
shift in the opponent's guiding perception. That is why, even
at a stage at which one is doing seme without being aware of
ki, the essence of seme still is ki.

I think that this level of combat is unknown in many disciplines (for example, judo, karate, or boxing) in which the
awareness of the practitioners is limited to the most directly
perceptible elements: speed, strength, aggressiveness, and so
on. This kind of combat represents a level of perception that

is difficult to stabilize in a combat of blows such as karate, but if practitioners of karate want to practice budo, they have no choice but to undertake this form of combat. Personally, my main concern is to draw attention to the possibility of applying this form of combat in the practice of karate.

8

Space in the Arts of Combat

As we have seen, the meaning of the word "ki" is broader than is implied by its usual translation, "vital energy." However, if we do focus on ki's dimension of vital energy, we can discriminate two types of bodily attitudes related to the sensation of ki.

The first of these is the one you can have when you contract as you compress the sensation of energy in your body. You contract the lower part of the belly by concentrating your attention there; or, if you are already advanced in karate, you can evoke the sensation you feel there when you perform the *sanchin* or *hangetsu* katas, in which you fill yourself with force by contracting your muscles. The objective at this point is not simply to contract the whole of the body but to integrate the general tensions of the body with the breath in order to generate the energetic body, the body that relates to technique.

In this situation in which the muscles are called into play in a forceful contraction, the sensation of ki is immediately present in a distinct way. At the same time, it is centripetal, that is, it is closed up in the body. Integrating the general tensions of the body requires a period of apprenticeship. It is not easy, but the first degree of this way of mobilizing ki is relatively easy to notice, even for people without much experience.

The second attitude is the one you can have when you release tension and relax and expand your physical sensation to the point where it diffuses into space. You feel the sensation of touching a distant tree, a mountain . . . your body becomes one with the air. In this situation, by contrast with the first, the sensation of your physical being is more vague and tends to dissolve in whatever your surroundings are.

The methods of strengthening ki in the martial arts integrate various elements that bring us back to these two attitudes; some of them give precedence to the first and others to the second. This is what creates the variety of methods. Even if the method being used is very balanced, it should not be applied in a mechanical fashion, because it is necessary to take into account the evolution and change of the person practicing the method. A man or woman who, at the beginning, makes the best use of the first form (contraction) will at a more advanced stage be best able to appreciate the second (release). The two types of elements coexist in varying proportions.

Nonetheless, in all the valid methods, as the person advances in the practice of the martial arts, the elements of release or relaxation take on ever greater importance.

Why?

The first form makes a suitable point of departure for the study of ki. It becomes in a certain way the core around which later, through relaxation of the body, you can develop a large sphere of awareness of energy, the sensation of which diffuses into space. However, if you limit yourself to practicing the method that focuses on contraction, it will be difficult to go beyond it to the advanced level. In fact, you will end up having acquired the tendency to persevere in the extreme exercise of muscular contraction, which will lead you to a certain type of impasse. In addition, as one grows older, one's metabolism changes, and this kind of contraction will bring out the weak points in your body, whereas other forms of exercises based on relaxation will allow improvement in your performance. This is why the application of methods has to vary according to age—the method is being applied by a person who is evolving and changing.

We often hear it said in certain karate schools in which the "hard" method is favored that practitioners are very strong until they reach forty, but as they approach fifty, they frequently encounter health problems. I have no statistics, so I cannot confirm this, but I share this impression in light of my own experience and observations.

On the basis of these preliminary considerations, I would like to advance the following hypothesis.

The combat of seme is based on the space projected by ki through the techniques employed by the combatants. The sensation of ki develops when the body is permeable to the sensation of the space that surrounds it, and it is easily masked when bodily sensation shrinks down as a result of a polarization of one's attention. Delicate or gentle contact with the skin accentuates the sensation of ki, whereas a hard or violent contact with the skin tends to prevent that sensation from developing.

We have seen that in kendo, the combatants face each other across a distance that develops and actualizes the sensation of ki.

In the practice of modern judo, you immediately find yourself body to body with your adversary, and you are dealing with a kind of physical contact in which pressure and force predominate. This form of combat almost does not require you to sharpen your ability to grasp the intention of your adversary across the space that separates you. Since you do not have enough time either to detect or to influence your adversary's intentions before entering into full bodily contact, it is difficult to cultivate ki of the second type. Combat in judo requires ki of the first type and allows you to strengthen it. But it is difficult to develop the other form of ki through this kind of combat, because the space into which you could extend your sensations is lacking.

In this regard, in jujutsu, the art from which judo is derived, the face-to-face begins at a distance, and there is more of a possibility of developing techniques based on ki in space. Jujutsu, the art of bare-handed combat of the warriors, was intended to be used against an adversary, armed or not. It involved the use of various weapons, such as blows from the fists and feet and various throws, locks, and holds, and therefore also a strategy from a distance as well as in contact.

In aikido, which is also derived from jujutsu, the techniques that were developed are based more on distance and evaluation of your opponent and early perception of an eventual attack, all of which favor the development of sensations of ki. However, the practice tends to diverge from the reality of combat, because there is a sense of cooperation between the two partners when they face off against each other. Thus the development of ki is oriented toward synchronization at the expense of the interplay that constitutes combat.

In this way, in relation to classical jujutsu, we can observe in judo and aikido two clearly distinct types of development or evolution in relation to the work on ki.

In karate combat, the space between the adversaries is as important as it is in kendo; it is possible to allow your awareness to enter this space and pick up the sensation of ki. But the immediacy of contact, as the combat continues and exchanges of technique take place, tends to prevent the combatants from placing their attention fully on what is articulating this space, even though they remain sensitive to actual changes in spatial distance. In a certain way, the very limited time span of the combat prevents the formation of a perception of ki. In addition, karate combat involves direct physical contact at the moment when technique is executed. Anticipation of this violent contact of bodies impels one to form a defensive body through muscle contraction gathering inward, and this tends to prevent the extension of sensitivity outward and to minimize the sensation of filling space.

Several forms of combat exist in karate. They vary according to the method and the style of the different schools. The classic form of karate without contact affords greater opportunity for developing sensitivity to ki, even though current versions of the art are far from exploiting this possibility.

In the full-contact form of combat, where the distance between the combatants is less than in the combat "without contact," the combatants anticipate violent physical contact from the start, and this tends to galvanize ki inside the body and prevent its diffusion outward. Therefore the possibility of opening to the sensation of ki is limited.

All the same, in karate, no matter what the form of combat is, the opportunity for the development of ki is virtually wide open, since the distance between the adversaries plays a role that is primordial for the combat.

Why has this possibility been developed so little in karate?

It is mainly because of a lack of awareness on the part of the practitioners of karate. The majority of them do not know that such a realm exists in combat. Combat has become a competition in which victory is decided by an external judge and not by a quality and a content that the combatants judge for themselves. They are not trained to acquire this kind of awareness. We could say that this is a deficiency in the culture of karate. If it is a deficiency, all that is necessary is to remedy it, because the possibility is wide open. But the system of a competitive sport is deeply rooted and presents itself for the majority of karate practitioners as the sole choice. That is why they are unaware of these possibilities. Comparison with kendo will clarify this point.

Compared to judo or karate, kendo offers greater opportunity to open to the sensation of ki, for two reasons. The space between combatants is more important because of the use of a weapon, the shinai. Anticipation of the shock of blows is less of a factor than in karate because of the use of protective armor, and this makes it possible not to close down the sensation of the body into a defensive attitude that becomes primary. When practicing with a wooden sword, the combatants do not touch each other, but they go to the limit of breaking the perimeter of security, which diminishes as the combatants advance in skill. Thus the practitioners can fully invest themselves in the space that separates them, without contracting their bodies in defense. Therefore this form of practice offers a better opportunity to cultivate the sensation of ki.

Thus it is in kendo that we can see the role of ki most concretely. In this respect, kendo is a privileged discipline. All the same, kendo seems formerly to have been much richer in physical techniques and to have had a much broader technical range than at present. In comparison to its tradition, the current model of kendo seems incomplete to me, especially concerning the general training of the body and the rules of combat. I think that contemporary practitioners cannot fail to become aware of these points if they look more deeply into the budo quality of kendo, kendo "as budo."

Practitioners of the martial arts, karate practitioners among others, can gain new reference points for their practice by studying the content of kendo "as budo," because it represents one of the most precious achievements of the practice of the Japanese warrior.

9

Ki, the Guide to Budo

We can say that it is at the moment when practitioners begin to feel the role of ki vividly that their combat practice tends to constitute itself as a way, and a true consciousness of budo begins to appear.

Why?

Feeling the role of ki vividly implies that the practitioner is practicing combat by trying to "strike after having won." It is not a matter of trying to win by landing a blow at any cost but of landing a blow with certainty. For practitioners, it is not a victory unless they strike after having won the battle of kizeme, that is to say, after having disconcerted their opponent to such a degree that the opponent has become vulnerable. By the same token, practitioners who have reached a certain level of accomplishment may feel that they have lost before receiving a single blow.

Thus what is necessary is to develop to a level of combat where the accuracy of this kind of sensation is confirmed by a blow delivered with complete certainty. A practitioner who has reached this level will attach maximal importance to that which underlies the combat, that is, to the combat of ki, the combat that takes place before an actual exchange of blows.

If you are disconcerted by your opponent's seme, his ki offensive, and you sketch a movement of defense in the void, it is because you have acted explicitly against that which is implicit, that is, you have responded to a mental phenomenon with a physical movement. In doing that, you have committed an error in your discernment of reality. If you become aware of this instantly, you feel a sense of dissociation in yourself, because your mind is not able to stop the body from making its erroneous gesture. If you sketch this futile movement, it is because your opponent has succeeded in making you move in spite of yourself. Therefore at this precise instant you have lost the possibility of taking the initiative and thus have lost without receiving a blow.

In kendo, the speed of the act of striking is many times increased by the use of a weapon, and the reflection of the situation described above is almost immediate, whereas in karate, where the technique is expressed directly through the body and the increase in speed due to the use of a weapon is absent, the action of attack is less rapid, and it is easier to recoup a time lag and correct an error. This is why conscious recognition of a mistaken movement that your opponent has succeeded in causing you to make in spite of yourself is less immediate, which precludes the learning process that would allow you to stabilize your mind in this respect.

In kendo combat, when your perception is open to the interplay of ki, losing in virtual combat is as important as receiving an actual blow. In this case, your problem becomes how to distinguish the real from the false, how to remain untroubled in the face of an offensive by your adversary either in the form of a movement or by means of ki.

When you are searching for an opportunity to attack your opponent, you perform seme in order to win the combat of sword points and make your opponent move the point of his sword out of the central line, his vital line. The opponent who allows an opening in spite of himself becomes vulnerable. At this instant, you deliver your blow, and you win an incontestable victory. You have created your victory; it is not a matter of chance or luck. When you score a hit by luck, if you are in a competition, the referee will say that you have won, but that will not satisfy you, because your adversary has remained unperturbed despite your blow, and, like you, he considers your victory of little value. In competition, the decision is in the hands of the referee, but this does not turn off the awareness of the combatants. If you are a sports competitor, you are satisfied with a decision in your favor, but if you are a budo practitioner, you will say to yourself, "I landed a blow, but my blow did not succeed in causing his mind to flicker." Your problem will then be how to cause a movement in the mind of the other through your ki.

In this way, the practitioner's focus progresses from a preoccupation with the simple technique of movement to working with a state of mind. Not letting yourself be disconcerted by seme and discriminating the false from the real in the actions of your opponent amount to acquiring penetrating insight that is sustained by strength of mind. Nonetheless, it would be wrong to say that there is a level where the mind alone is the determining force, because without physical technique, there is no combat.

Budo has a twofold structure: it is necessary to be prepared at every moment to unleash your violence, but it is also necessary to maintain a state of lucidity so that the mind can fully perceive what is happening around you. Such lucidity makes it possible for you to transform your own aggression into mobilizable potential in a state of tranquillity. A poem by Miyamoto Musashi conveys this state of mind:

> The current of the winter river
> reflects the moon
> on the transparent water like a mirror.

The notion of plunging your hand into freezing and rapidly moving water evokes a cold that cuts like the blade of a sword. The current is also there—the dynamism of combat. At the same time, the surface of the water gives the appearance of purity and calm. If the surface is disturbed, the moon will be broken into pieces. This poem, which is frequently quoted to describe the state of mind in sword combat, does in fact show the two sides that compose it, the violence and the calm. A reader who does not practice budo will no doubt feel the beauty of the uncompromising coldness of the image; a practitioner will perceive in the depths of this image the sensation of burning force. This is the difference between communication through words and communication through the body. This difference is more than cultural; it will also be present among Japanese readers depending on whether or not they are practitioners.

At the elementary level of combat, especially when one is young, a combatant acting aggressively and violently has a good chance of scoring a victory. But the level of combat envisaged by budo involves a longer time frame. It brings into play a variety of human faculties that remain dormant in the ordinary state but can be developed over time. As a result, in order to reach a high level in budo, we have to travel a long road, and the form of combat we come to is different from the combat of our youth. If you are sixty or seventy years of age, you cannot fight effectively in the same way as when you were twenty.

This difference corresponds to an improvement in the mastery of the technique and of oneself. The stage envisaged is one where mind is reflected in the technique in the most acute way. At this point, we become receptive to something in the depths of our consciousness that earlier on was masked by the impetuosity of action. That is to say, as soon as you think of striking a blow and hurting your opponent, the superego whispers that this is not right. This whisper, as tiny as it might be, is big enough to put the brakes on the spontaneity of your act, and you have just enough detachment to feel this. I believe that this is the meaning of the saying "If the mind is just, the sword is just; if the mind is not just, the sword is not just." This maxim is often interpreted in a moral way, but it is technical in origin. The art of combat is a pragmatic art. I would say that morality derives here from a pragmatism pushed to the limit. This is the particular quality of budo. It has nothing to do with associating moral values with the practice of weaponry.

Combat is an ascetic and introspective activity that is capable of causing confusion.

Relentless and impassioned repetitive training has a suitable place to the extent that it is part of the logic of a martial art that has a broader sense. It fits into a psychological structure that has been built up over time in a tradition; you are not training blindly or at random. If you were training simply to be able to fight, and if you never thought of anything else besides fighting, and the point of the fighting were simply to destroy others, this would be an abnormal situation. But the logic of training has a sense, and if a person does not see it, the all-out training referred to above can be qualified as abnormal or obsessive.

When you engage in combat, you plunge into the problems of ego, but not in just any old way. For example, those who are passionately dedicated to winning are carried along by a will to dominate others in order to affirm themselves. If this will leads them to enter into the logic of budo, they will discover, paradoxically, that this will to dominate can be satisfied only if it allows itself to disappear. Encountering again and again in the process of practice the contradiction between this desire for realization on the part of their ego and the effacement of this desire that is necessary to actually achieve the goal, they will be led to a profound reexamination of themselves.

In kendo, the practitioner enters into this logic rather rapidly, because this tradition and the way it is practiced call into question the supremacy of physical strength and the exuberant energy of youth. Young practitioners, even if they are very gifted in combat, will gain this experience by going through a large number of matches with practitioners of different levels. But in the other martial arts, such as karate, practitioners lose their youthful strength and then often give up their martial arts practice well before reaching the stage just described. The methods of training usually practiced in karate are mainly based on the first buoyant resilient strength of youth. In the forms of combat that do not use protective equipment and involve the direct striking of blows, robust strength and the ability to bounce back assure a certain supremacy over older combatants. This situation allows the impression to develop that the ideal, model practice of the art is one in which dynamic and spectacular techniques based on strength and rapidity of movement predominate. In addition, on the whole there are no older practitioners or teachers who are truly capable of dominating in free combat. This reinforces the same image and fails to open perspectives favoring a higher vision of the techniques of combat.

Later on, toward the age of thirty-five or forty, we begin to experience a reduction in the quality of our physical condition. In kendo, this is the moment when practitioners enter the most meaningful and intensive phase of the practice, because they become sensitive to the problem of ki in a real way and begin to adjust their approach to combat so as to shape it as budo. At this same moment, the majority of karate practitioners have little inclination to persevere, because those who have practiced combat seriously have accumulated various traumas, and because the model they have learned gives them very little room to adapt to advancing age. Therefore they quit or reduce their level of training, contenting themselves for the most part with the practice of kata, in which combat remains virtual. However, combat in budo is never virtual.

If you are trying to act spontaneously and accurately, it is necessary to free the mind from the fetters of consciousness; this is where the teaching concerning an empty mind comes from. At this level, the effort to increase your efficiency ends up in a kind of paradox; for if you want to defeat your opponent (which in the technical sense means to kill him) in the surest possible way, it is necessary not to want to defeat (kill) him. You must become detached from winning if you want to win. This takes us close to the maxim "One must prepare to die if one wants to survive."

In this way, the activity of combat leads to a process of introspection and fundamental questioning that takes you in the direction of a reorganization of the personality, a reorganization that aims at making you more penetrating in your judgment, capable of not allowing yourself to be perturbed, capable of acting spontaneously and accurately and being able to draw on your greatest abilities. The process of this reorganization is the training that contains the striving toward self-development that constitutes budo.

We could say that budo is the product of a paradox created by the pragmatism of the Japanese martial arts pushed to its limit. This is because from the moment when practitioners become aware of what is happening in their minds, their goal, as I have just explained, begins to shift toward a study of the nature of combat. The focus of their preoccupations formerly was: how many enemies have you killed? It now becomes: how did you defeat your adversary without killing him?

The sword, which was originally intended to kill the enemy (*setsunin ken*), transforms stage by stage, as the idea of seme is born and then stabilizes, into "the sword that makes a man live" (*katsunin ken*). The sword makes a man live by strengthening awareness of the weight of his being. The idea of modern budo is the development of this thought.

Through this sort of bird's-eye view of the evolution of a practitioner's consciousness, we are able to understand that it is at the moment when practitioners become aware of the importance of that which is ordinarily invisible that their subjective education begins. This "something" is the key to budo. It is ki. In other words, as long as people remain unaware of the sensation of ki in the practice of the martial arts and do not arrive at reshaping their practice through a fundamental reexamination of their being, they will not be able to pursue the path of self-development properly, since they will be traveling on a dark path without illumination.

10

Ma, the Spatial Concretization of Ki

*T*he essence of combat is *ma*" is a famous dictum from the teaching of Ito Ittosai (flourished in the sixteenth and seventeenth centuries), the founder of the Itto Ryu (the Itto school). He also said:

"If you think too much about the ma, you will be incapable of reacting appropriately to change. If you do not think about it, the ma will be right, even in a situation of movement. That is why it is necessary not to attach your mind to the ma; you must not create the ma in your mind. It must be like the reflection of the moon on water. If your mind is as clear as the cloudless sky, you will be like water reflecting the moon, no matter what the situation is."

All the masters, like Ittosai, stress the importance of the ma. This term is usually translated as "distance, separation, interval, gap in space," but it also means "temporal interval, psychological flow." It is strongly linked to the notion of cadence, because ma also means "interval between the cadences." In Japanese architecture, ma has a double meaning. As a unit of measure, it refers to the regular interval that separates posts.

In a broader sense, it qualifies each room in terms of the accommodation it provides for various uses (*kyakuma*, area for guests; *ima*, daily living area for the family).

What is the ma?

The ma is a space into which human beings project their ki and thus circumscribe the effect that space has on various interactions that take place within it. The projection of ki becomes stable through harmonizing itself with other elements. Thus in traditional architecture, living space is set up in such a way that people feel at ease with each other and their environment. This is done by seeking a balance in the planned space, the elements of construction, and surrounding nature.

For example, in the ma of the tea ceremony, the people preparing and drinking tea work together toward developing harmony with all the objects that surround them in the space intended for that purpose. When a tea ceremony is performed in natural surroundings, certain makeshift elements are sometimes put in place—pieces of fabric or a rope. Is this not because people feel the need to provide a framework for the gestures and actions in which they invest their ki? If the ki is allowed to diffuse into the unbounded natural environment, the tea ceremony fails to reach its full fruition, because the activity of the people performing it is a crystallization of ki within a precise form.

In this sense, the act of performing a tea ceremony is fundamentally different from that of drinking tea at a picnic in the open space of nature. The nature of the sensation of pleasure experienced is also different. When you drink tea at a picnic, you feel the pleasure of freedom along with the feeling of having no physical or visual constraints. As a result, your ki floats like a bird flying free. When you drink tea in a tea ceremony, you feel profound calm and tranquillity, not because you are in the silence of nature but because your ki has structured itself through a form of gestural and spatial tranquillity carried out in a preconceived space.

If you have had the experience of training in a martial art in the immense hall of a modern gymnasium and also in a dojo of classical dimensions, have you not vividly felt the difference in your spatial ambience? You make the same technical movements, but the sensation is not the same. Why? Over the course of time, the architecture of the classical dojo has acquired the dimensions that appropriately fit the ki of the people practicing their discipline in it.

Thus behind the phenomenon of the ma lies the particular fashion in which human beings are expressing themselves, affirming themselves, or testing themselves, by manifesting their physical existence through a sensibility that goes beyond it.

When Ittosai says, "If you think too much about the ma, you will be incapable of reacting appropriately to change. If you do not think about it, the ma will be right, even in a situation of movement," his idea of the ma goes beyond a speculative, conceptual understanding. For him, the ma is an extension of the body. When you expand your bodily sensation into the space that surrounds you, you will feel the intention and the action of your opponent "as water reflects the moon."

The sensitivity that perceives ki is obscured by speculative effort. It is in this sense that the practice of ki comes close to Zen meditation, which aims at the realization of nonthought. It is a fact that the development of the sensation of ki is strongly dependent upon one's mental attitude. If you see your arm, your hand, or your fingers, your body takes shape in terms of the appropriate name given to each body part. In this way, you conceive of your body rationally, which is very different from feeling it "as though" you were touching a distant mountain. The sensation of the expansion of the body is beyond verbal rationality. Thus the nature of mental activity is different in the activity of verbal speculation and in the exercise of developing ki. In other words, in the exercise of ki, we must go beyond the semantic limitation of language. The use of images is more effective than the use of words.

For these reasons, we may think of ma as a spatial concretization of ki.

11

Detect and Conceal

Prior to the exchanges of combat technique, there is the combat of ki, invisible to the eyes of third parties. High-level kendo practitioners appreciate this invisible combat, the combat of the stage that precedes the gestural confrontations. Indeed, the most important combat takes place when the combatants are facing off against each other and pointing their weapons. The ki of one combatant interacts with the ki of the other, and this manifests as slight movements in their bodies and their weapons. Uninitiated spectators will be irritated by this apparent lack of movement that goes on for too long, whereas the adepts present will deeply appreciate the virtual exchange of attack and defense, the combat of ki.

The novice spectators begin to enjoy things when the two combatants execute movements of attack and defense. But the exchange of technique by high-level practitioners is generally brief, since it is the result of a long combat of ki. By contrast, the exchanges of technique by young students of average or low level, who are not yet quite capable of performing the combat of ki, are more turbulent, varied, and dynamic. This provides more enjoyment for the spectators.

Thus budo combat of superior quality hardly makes a good show for the general public, which is only aware of explicit movements. But it is the public's appreciation that counts for the organizers of martial arts shows. This is one of the main reasons that martial arts of high quality are hard to present to the public. Consequently public opinion is shaped by people who appreciate martial arts presentations without having any idea of the superior level of the practice. The activities of a sports federation, which is based on the common level of practice, respond directly to this type of public opinion, and, spurred by its growing need for members, the organization itself ends up promoting the transformation of the martial arts into the stuff of shows. This being the case, it seems all but impossible for high quality in the martial arts to be pursued within the context of such federations. The pursuit of quality in the martial arts is fundamentally a personal matter.

The combat of budo is above all the combat of ki. Ki emanates from the two combatants, and both of them direct it against their adversaries. The one who is weaker will be overwhelmed and defeated. But the combat of ki unfolds in a complex fashion. When your opponent attempts to push you with his ki, you can either face him directly and project yours toward him, or you can conceal your ki in order to conceal your intention. In this situation, if your opponent attacks you but fails to disturb your ki, you have the opportunity to make a counterattack. This is because you will have clearly seen the moment when he unleashed his attack, since his intention to attack reflected off you as you remained alert and ready. If your opponent is skillful, he also will conceal his ki in order to get to see your reaction; then he will project his ki toward you, then project it a little more, while taking the measure of your responses. . . . You will do the same thing, and the combat of ki will continue in this fashion.

If you launch an attack with a strong onslaught of ki, your opponent might feel this and be able to anticipate and overpower your attack; at that point you run the risk of losing. That is why it is important to learn to emit your ki to repulse an opponent and, at the same time, to learn to be able to conceal it. To strike without emitting ki is called "the blow of nonthought" or "the blow of concealed intention."

There is a Japanese expression, "cover up the *kehai*," which means "hold back the emanation of ki" or "conceal your ki." This was one of the basic points in the education of Japanese warriors, who sometimes had to be very discreet in front of their lords, as though they were not there. This technique was developed and applied in the field of espionage.

From your living body, emanate the ki that you have developed more or less through your exercises. You detect the ki of the other person by means of your own ki. Ki is like a radar emission. The combat of ki is often similar to that between a submarine and a torpedo boat. The boat on the hunt searches for the submarine with sonar rays. The submarine hides, covers all signs of life, the hunter detects it. . . . In combat, we use forms of ki by which you push your opponent back, you detect his intention, you conceal yourself.

Mind guides ki, but this is not a speculative activity. There is sometimes a shadow of speculation during combat, but if you enlarge this shadow, you risk falling behind in your timing, because speculation is a fetter on spontaneous movement. The movement that is spontaneously right is guided by ki. And ki is guided by a mind that is at one with a total and diffuse physical sensation. It is in this way that, if the combat of budo is the combat of ki, it is also a combat of the mind. This is the context in which this teaching shines: "If the mind is right, the sword is right."

12

The Combat of Ki

In this way, by opening our perception to the combat of ki, we are able to penetrate into the realm of mental combat and, through this, to develop an understanding of the combat of budo.

From the moment we attempt to raise the quality of our combat by activating ki, our perception of combat takes a big step forward.

The most direct questions about combat are: "In what situation does your attack technique succeed? In what situation does it fail? In what situation do you win? In what situation do you lose?" You can try to understand and to answer these questions by analyzing situations in terms of movements. But you will never be able to get a satisfactory answer through analysis of physical movements alone, even though analysis of this sort remains indispensable for improving the quality of your technique on the gestural level. But these movements are endless in number, and it is not possible to get to the core of your problems on the basis of elements as variable as these. What is necessary is to touch directly upon that which gives birth to the various gestural situations. Combat takes on the structure that it does by following ki, consciously or not. Strategy may be guided by a calculation, but it is by being guided by ki in the moment of combat, which is something that happens in the dark, that you modulate the forms of your movement. Therefore what is necessary is to perceive the variable situations of combat through the principle of ki.

For example, as we saw earlier, if a feint succeeds, it is because the ki of your opponent was moved. If you are unable to cause a movement in the ki of your opponent, no feint will work. For this reason, it is not fruitful to examine the gestural forms of feints and to increase the number of your reference points: that only serves to complicate situations by giving the impression of analyzing your problems objectively. These processes are traps for your view of method in the martial arts. Despite this, we find a great number of examples of this type of approach in works on the subject that call themselves "scientific."

All that is needed is to understand a simple principle: your attack will succeed if you implement it after having troubled the ki of your opponent; you will suffer his attack if your ki is disturbed by him. There is the essence of the problem. With this as a basis, you can examine the process of your training: how can you unbalance the ki of your opponent and how can you avoid having your own ki unbalanced by him? That will become the central focus of your training.

Here is an example taken from my work *Miyamoto Musashi*:

Shirai Toru (1783–1850) is considered one of the greatest adepts of the last two centuries. Katsu Kaishu (1823–1899), a famous statesman of the Meiji period, an accomplished practitioner of the way of the sword and of Zen, describes as follows the impression that he had of Shirai Toru while training with him:

"The way of the sword and Zen are identical, any difference residing only in words and forms. When I dedicated myself to the way of the sword, I had the opportunity to take lessons from an adept named Shirai Toru. I learned an enormous amount from him. His art of the sword had a kind of supernatural power. As soon as he took up the sword, there emanated from him an atmosphere that was at once austere and pure, then an insuperable potency surged forth from the end of his sword, which was supernatural. I was unable even to stand and face him. I wanted to reach his level and underwent serious training, but to my sorrow, I was very far away from it. One day I asked him why I felt the fear that I did before his sword. He then replied with a smile as follows:

"'It is because you have made some progress in the sword. He who has nothing will feel nothing. See how profound the sword is.'

"These words further increased my terror before the vastness of the way of the sword."

In fact, the outpouring of Shirai Toru's energy in combat was such that the adepts of the period used to say, "Shirai's sword of gives off a sphere of luminosity." For Katsu Kaishu, the strange energy given off by the sword of Shirai was the equivalent of the energy one can obtain through Zen.

The last words of Shirai Toru quoted above make it possible for us to understand why a beginner who has no experience of combat can sometimes act in an effective and courageous manner. As the proverb says, "The blind man has no fear of the snake." People who do not recognize the danger of a situation can sometimes show surprising courage. They astonish themselves in retrospect when they realize what they have done. Over the long course of the path of practicing the activity of combat, there will be many corrections, many lessons learned.

Here is a very ordinary example that we encounter frequently.

The feint of an attack will have no effect whatever on a person who has never received a blow. Such a person is able to behave lucidly because the feint does not recall to him any memory of pain or arouse any fear. As a result, he is capable of acting as if the feint had never occurred, and this will permit him to act in exactly the wrong way (from the point of the view of the opponent) to the opponent's tactic. He will be in a position to deliver an effective blow. He may even go so far as to think that he is stronger than his opponent and of superior skill.

Over the course of practice, he will accumulate experiences of receiving blows, sometimes violent ones. Once he has this experience, when he faces an adversary, he will react with sensitivity to the movements of a feint. Feints will evoke the pain of blows and thus will arouse fear. He will be defeated by a person whom he had considered not as strong as himself. Thus as he enters the next phase of his development, he might think he is actually regressing. Some practitioners give up the practice at this point and others continue. Progress in budo is far from linear.

The situation is similar when it comes to the combat of ki. If your sensitivity to ki has not been built up, you will be unable to perceive a ki offensive. As a result, you might sometimes act more bravely than is sensible. Even if the opponent is a very accomplished practitioner, you will not have the impression that you are losing for as long as you have yet to receive a blow. Once your perception has developed enough, you will feel the pressure of ki. This is the way Katsu Kaishu was overpowered, and his master characterized the situation very well: "It is because you have made some progress."

13

The Meaning and the Value of Combat

Is the sole result of being capable of carrying on the combat of ki an increase in your effectiveness in combat? It is certainly true that developing the sharpness and accuracy of your ki enables you to fight better, but does the fact of being able to fight better have any significance outside of combat itself? If it only leads to being able to wipe out an opponent more efficiently, it has no more importance than any other element of skill. And in that case, the combat of ki amounts to no more than a subtle form of combat and physical know-how.

I will take up and develop an idea I discussed earlier from a different angle.

Seme is the act of perturbing the ki of your opponent. If you succeed in perturbing the ki of your opponent, that is to say, if you succeed in seme, your attack will succeed. Where your attack succeeds without your having deployed seme, it is just a matter of luck. Seme is the action by which you obtain a sure victory.

You attempt to upset the ki of your opponent and at the same time you keep your own ki fully harmonized. If your ki is upset, you will feel something unpleasant, sometimes a gap in the synchronization of your rhythm, sometimes a disturbance in your breathing. If, on top of this unpleasant sensation of your ki being upset, you are hit, the only thing you can do is admit your defeat by bowing to your opponent. This experience will allow you to strengthen your ki later, because in examining the moment when you received the blow and the way in which you received it—which amounts to an auto-critique—you can learn how to remedy your inadequacy. If you succeed in your seme and attack, this will also strengthen your ki by stabilizing your sense of the relationship between the sensation of ki and action.

In this way, the combat of ki permits the two opponents to mutually strengthen their ki. This is the hidden part of the quest for effectiveness in combat. Through this mutual reinforcement of ki, the practice takes on a dual sense. The first aspect is clear: strengthening the body, developing the capacity to carry on combat on the subtle level. What is the second?

The strengthening of ki is linked with an increase in vitality. This aspect coincides with the methodology of kiko, the practice of working with the breath or working with energy. But there is something else here that touches on the moral aspect of our existence.

Disturbance in your ki is most often felt as an unpleasant sensation. Thus you can keep it from happening by avoiding certain unpleasant sensations, such as fear, anxiety, hesitation, doubt, and also anger, hatred, disgust—in short, the sources of stress that, it is said, speaking another kind of language, increase the negative ki. By contrast, relaxation, calmness linked with a peaceful mind, and smiling increase ki, that is, they increase the positive ki.

Any kind of thought or idea that might become the object of an inner moral conflict is capable of producing a disturbance in your ki. We know that in many cases, even when we are not entirely aware of it, the body acts or produces a variety of symptoms on the basis of subconscious perceptions. Ki manifests immediately, as soon as the body reacts, even before it produces visible symptoms.

The body has a system of resistance against whatever is harmful to it, and before it produces clear outward signs of problems, its ki is disturbed in a way that can be perceived by a person who has developed a highly sensitized awareness of ki. Chinese medicine is based on this correlation between ki and bodily afflictions; it tries to bring about healing by restoring the balance of ki. The awareness of ki in the art of combat does not necessarily go this far, but the link to this approach to ki is very easy to see.

Practitioners of kendo, in the early stages, as is the case with the other disciplines of combat, attain effectiveness through being aggressive, letting themselves be carried along by the energy of emotions. But in the high level of kendo combat, the least movement of the mind, especially if it is based on a fairly strong emotion such as hatred, fear, or doubt, runs the risk of producing a disturbance of ki. The penalty will be a decrease in effectiveness. For kendo practitioners, the development of awareness on this level comes around the sixth or seventh *dan*. Practitioners then understand that they cannot fight well if they allow themselves to be carried away by violence or aggression, that their burning energy must be guided by a calm mind. Starting at this level, ki guides practitioners who enter a realm in which their practice will progressively become one with the way. This is what constitutes the very special quality of the discipline of kendo.

In the other disciplines of combat, this possibility is greatly reduced, and combat goes on in the dimension of violence, where the person who is the most aggressive has the greatest chance of carrying off the victory.

Thus *yi chuan*, boxing based on *yi* (thought or intention), trains its practitioners to a state of artificial or technical insanity so as to activate their potentialities for combat to the ultimate possible degree. In the exercise of *zhan zhuang* (meditation in a fixed posture), you train yourself to develop a state of mind that has influence over your body. At one point in this exercise, you imagine yourself surrounded by ferocious animals, for example, a tiger opening its jaws or a snake with a venomous glance, or you see yourself being approached by your mortal enemies. You imagine a situation in which you are being attacked by these beings you hate and fear the most, and you crush them. The result is that you secrete an abundance of adrenaline, and your body is stimulated to its most combative state. By repeating this exercise every day for years, you can form and fortify a nervous system that is adapted for combat. In the system of yi chuan, there are several instructions for relaxation so that you can calm yourself in order to establish a state of balance. However, for combat, there is no alternative—the effectiveness of this method is purely based on this explosive force that is built upon a state of technical and artificial insanity, on the human power that is closest to that of an animal.

Yo Yongnien, one of the students of Wang Xiangzhai, the founder of yi chuan, told me the following: "When Master Wang emitted his explosive force, his face transformed completely. I never saw such a terrible human face in my life. This is hard to imagine when you see the peaceful face he has in his photos, don't you find?"

There is no doubt that among the methods developed in the tradition of the martial arts, the method of yi chuan is one that is effective in developing the faculties of combat.

Being sensitive to ki means perceiving one's mental state by means of a physical sensation. We find in this a kind of morality that is not of a religious type but one that is inherent in our body and flows directly from it. Effectiveness in combat is, by nature, aggressive and destructive; in a society where confrontations are rarely physical, this has to be legitimated. In order to create the equivalent of a sheath for the cutting edge of the sword, a morality is necessary that flows spontaneously from the technique and from the body. This is where ki becomes important. In a certain way, the objective of budo is to find a way to develop a moral body, and this is what distinguishes it from the many disciplines of combat. This is what allows it to offer us the possibility of finding a superior dimension in the practice of a physical discipline.

14

The Classical Methods of Developing Ki in Combat

*I*t goes without saying that the combat of budo is not an abstraction. It seeks to find a way to be effective. Getting into a deeper dimension of combat through ki makes it possible, on the one hand, to increase the effectiveness of combat and, on the other, to extend practice over the long term, in fact, through one's entire lifetime. In kendo, it is not rare to find masters who practice right up to the time of their death while continuing to have extraordinary abilities at their disposal. In the bare-handed martial arts, for example, in karate, it is very rare to find a master practicing combat after the age of sixty. However, in a discipline like *taiki ken*, where the use of ki is central, the late Kenichi Sawai continued to practice bare-handed combat very effectively, bringing to bear abilities of a very high order, until just before his death at the age of almost eighty.

As I see it, work on ki is present, explicitly or implicitly, in the disciplines of budo in which the practitioners are able to travel a long path, continuing to improve their abilities all along the way. In kendo, work on ki comes into play after a certain level and in taiki ken, from the very beginning. In certain schools of jujutsu and of *kenjutsu*, work on ki is not stressed, but it is present implicitly.

Attaining Ki by the Method of Kata

This first method is based on training in technique and its application by means of repetition. This is the method in most general use.

For example, in learning kendo, you begin with the correct handling of the shinai; in karate, you begin by learning the precise forms for punches and kicks. In combat, you cannot get an *ippon* (knockout) if you do not strike correctly. You train yourself to develop the capacity to carry on a superior level of combat with magnificent technique. Just scoring hits any old way is totally out of the question.

Today if you analyze the recommended techniques of kendo, it is possible to select and standardize a number of model techniques in which the practitioner needs to be thoroughly trained. These model moves represent a kind of ideal technique for the practitioner to assimilate. Even though they are not usually referred to by the term "kata," they do present the structure and characteristics of kata. We may draw the conclusion that there are kata implicit in kendo combat. In the basic training of kendo, *jigeiko*, practitioners work using these models as criteria for the right and wrong ways to execute movements in combat. The same is true for practitioners of karate.

In karate, you train with combat techniques that can be put directly to use: series of technical moves, footwork, and so on. It is possible almost to standardize a body of useful and necessary movements for the forms of combat that you practice every day. You can almost form kata with these movements, but you will come up with a set of kata that is different from the ones designated as traditional. The same thing could be said for judo.

In any case, you do not train for combat just any old way. You train following a model that approaches a certain level of perfection. If you perform a thousand striking exercises with the shinai (*suburi*), this means repeating the movement a thousand times, trying to come closer and closer to the perfect strike. When you exercise in this way, repeating a technique in accordance with an idealized model, this is the method of kata in the broad sense of the term. The reason people do not actually call this the kata method is that qualification of kata is customarily attributed to movements established by tradition. But if we analyze the dynamic inherent in the development of the kata, it turns out that at the time each kata was formed and established, it was being practiced in the same way as you practice movements today that are useful, necessary, and even indispensable for the development of your technical capacity for combat. It never had anything at all to do with a kind of gestural ceremonialism, and the gap that exists now between the traditional kata and the actual practice of combat remains to be justified.

Jigeiko is a process of assimilating the elements necessary to carry on the most perfect combat. But it is not enough merely to execute a perfect movement; what is necessary is to execute it in a combat situation, face-to-face with an opponent. You cannot perform well in combat just by chance.

When you do reach the point of performing satisfactorily, it is because you have been able to feel a sort of fullness in scoring an ippon. In this situation, prior to striking your blow, you have created an instance of vulnerability in your opponent, because you have succeeded in disturbing his guard and his mind. Your attack was based precisely on this emptiness in your opponent at a moment when you yourself were filled with energy. This result is produced by the right posture of your body as you move your sword through the right trajectory. The same holds true in the combat of karate, just replacing the sword blow with a punch or a kick.

It is in this situation that you can feel a fullness. In this case, it is because, even without being conscious of it, you were guided by the sensation of a certain something, and you acted placing your confidence in this sensation. At the moment of striking your blow, you had a sensation of becoming one with this certain something. This is the sensation of ki. The sensation of ki is present in the sensation of perfect execution of technique in the course of combat.

In exercising with kata, this sensation is modulated to relate with a technical form. When you study the classical kata, you find that they contain the necessary elements for attaining a superior level of combat. Many kata have been distorted in the process of transmission, but at the moment when a kata is formed, it displays an idealized state of a technique that is effective as a means of training for combat. The idealized state of the technique corresponds to the highest level of the technique, that level at which the physical technique and your state of mind become one. Your ki must circulate naturally in this state. We could say that training in a technique in this manner corresponds to a principle of energy. If a technical movement is perfect, it is because it is in harmony with the effectiveness that adjusts your ki to a technical form. The perfect form of a technique that is not effective makes no sense, just as there cannot exist a perfect sword that does not cut.

We have seen that the term "ki" refers to a range of sensations that is vague and quite vast. In budo, we utilize ki by modulating it to adjust to a technical form. When we say about a master, "No matter what movements he makes, they constitute perfect technique," this is precisely because he is capable of following his ki, not in a literal way but in a way that is profoundly technical. He has integrated his technique so completely that his movements are in conformity with the principle that underlies technique in the broader sense of kata. This is what we call going beyond form by learning form, going beyond the kata by penetrating deeply into the kata.

The kata shows a model combat technique developed into a perfect form; it is an invitation to climb to the summit and a guide for reaching it. Thus the kata is based on a system in which knowledge is situated at a high point and practitioners are attempting to raise themselves to that level. The technical form is a means of climbing up, for it is not an end in itself. The goal of the kata is to go beyond the kata.

When practitioners observe what is going on in their mind during a strenuous training session in which they are attempting to improve their technique, they encounter the image of their master, the person who showed or taught them the technique. Their movements are associated with an image of perfection represented by the master, especially when they are exercising by themselves. In the course of the training process, practitioners exert themselves to do as well as their elders, as well as their master; later they desire to surpass him, to defeat him. The heavier this image of the master is, the more it haunts them. Struggling against this image is the process of training—repetition. This psychological linkage is characteristic of the application of the methodology of kata.

A better understanding of the logic inherent in the kata method and its connection with ki helps us to advance in our comprehension and practice of budo. To do this, it is indispensable to know how to look at and work with kata from a different point of view. The kata is not simply a standardized technique. It is not a mold, not a ceremony, not an imaginary combat. Kata is a method that requires several keys to allow it to unfold completely. I will develop this idea further later on.

Strengthening Ki through the Method of Energy

The second method works in more or less the reverse way. It aims from the beginning to strengthen that which is the vehicle of effectiveness—ki. I would say that this method seeks to reorganize the sensory system in such a way as to allow the body to function spontaneously with a better way of regulating energy. If the first method is based on technical forms developed in the hope of attaining perfection, the second is based directly on the sensory system inherent in the most highly efficient and effective movements of the technique.

This is the reason, according to this method, that the technique should arise spontaneously on the basis of the sensation of ki. It is not based on the process of learning specific techniques as the kata method is. If there is a development of technique, it will come after one has attained sufficient mastery of ki. *Taiki ken*, which is derived from the Chinese method of yi chuan, is a typical example of this approach.

In the art of the sword, a minimum of technical mastery is obligatory, enough to know how to use the sword's cutting edge. This is true even for this method that takes the opposite approach of the method of kata and seeks to train a practitioner for combat directly through the acquisition of the essential mental and energetic factor. The method of Hirayama Gyozo (1759–1828) is a good example of this method, since here the learning of technique was reduced to a minimum. His method consisted of a single technique: an exercise for two combatants in which one armed with a long shinai attacked an opponent who wore a protective covering on his head and was armed with a short shinai of forty centimeters. The role of the latter combatant was to attack and strike his opponent in the chest with the aim of running him through, and he had to do this regardless of what blows he might receive while closing in.

Hirayama Gyozo wrote in one of his works, *Commentary on the Sword (Kensetsu)*: "The object of the art of the sword is to kill the enemy. The essence of it is to cause your lethal mind to penetrate the chest of your adversary."

The school of Hirayama Gyozo was called Sinkan Ryu (literally, the pervaded-by-mind school) or Shinnuki Ryu (the pervaded-by-the-essence school). According to Hirayama Gyozo, if your mind pervades your adversary, you are victorious, and that is the surest and most effective method in real combat with the sword. I see in this a process of working with energy that seeks to strengthen the mind in the most direct manner. The simplicity of this training is the repetition of a single gesture, which is comparable with the apparently simple exercise of standing without moving in standing Zen, *ritsu zen*. However, with the stationary posture of *ritsu zen*, you exercise your mind with the intention of creating a mental and physical state disposed toward crushing your opponent, whoever that may be. In combat with the sword, you have to be able to use the sword correctly—that is why the simple exercise of suburi is the basis for the method of Hirayama Gyozo. His method consists in executing this simple gesture and in strengthening the most fundamental factor in combat. Therefore I would characterize it as a method that aims at strengthening in a direct and simple manner the essence of practical energy: the ki of combat.

In the tradition of the sword, a method that focuses on energy is most often applied in tandem with the method of kata or after the latter has been completed. I will take the examples of two famous masters of the nineteenth century, Shirai Toru (1783–c. 1845) and Yamaoka Tesshu (1836–1888), who took this approach.

The problems encountered by these two adepts are problems that any reflection on the methodology of the Japanese martial arts must reckon with.

During the second half of his life, Shirai Toru dominated his opponents by means of the strange power that emanated from his sword. It is said that the tip of his *bokken* emitted a sphere of luminosity. Before he reached this level, he encountered an obstacle that he was able to surmount only through

long years of training and ascetic meditation. He condensed
the process he had gone through into a method—the fortifi-
cation of energy, *rentan*. This is based mainly on a process of
working with energy that corresponds in large part to the
martial kiko practiced today. According to Shirai Toru,
rentan is the only concrete method there is for attaining the
superior level of the way of the sword.

Yamaoka Tesshu also attained an extraordinary level in
the art of the sword by dedicating himself to the practice of
Zen. He was poor and, toward the age of thirty, was living in
a house that was in bad condition. He had received the nick-
name Tetsu Clothed in Rags, but also another, Tetsu, the
Demon of the Dojo. A number of his friends recounted that
at night, the ceiling of his house was alive with the sound of
mice, but as soon as Tetsu began doing *zazen*, his ki filled the
space and the mice stopped making noise. It would also happen that numbers of them would fall off the beams they were
running on. After several years had passed, when Tesshu would
begin zazen, the mice would stop running around and come
down to where he was and play around him. Of course, I can't
vouch for the authenticity of this story.

In any case, there are many accounts concerning the power
of Tesshu's ki. Takano Sazaburo (1862–1950), one of the
greatest masters of the early part of the twentieth century,
tells us the following story:

> During training, the Master had his students strike
> him, but they never got the feeling of actually touch-
> ing him. When I tried to hit him with a heavy blow, I
> always found the point of the master's shinai at my

throat. . . . The attitude of the Master was like that of a ball that can never be made to fall over. He had an unfathomable suppleness, unfathomable because his suppleness contained the power of steel. So it happened during training that even if I hit him right in the center of his head (*men*), I could never get the feeling that I had touched him. Everybody was overcome by his ki. . . . Even when the point of his shinai would get no closer than thirty centimeters in front of me, if he made a small movement with the point, I always had the impression of receiving a blow to the throat (*tsuki*). The Master did not manipulate his sword with his hands but with his energy center. . . . It happened that one day I received a light tsuki strike, and at that moment, I did not feel anything. But as I was returning home, I was overcome by a strange sensation, as though my throat had a hole in it and the outside air were circulating inside. This strange sensation lasted for two days.

These two great masters were able to radically transform the quality of their sword, one by means of rentan, the other through zazen, and we may conclude that these practices helped them to reorganize the manner of feeling and acting that underlay their technique of the sword. From a practical point of view, those who practice with this method do not necessarily think that they are engaged in any reorganization. Subjectively, they may feel a sense of moral improvement or, depending on their beliefs, a sense of illumination or of purification of mind and body. But what is very likely common to everybody is a strong sensation of ki.

If it is true that Zen influenced the Japanese practice of the sword, it did not do so as a speculative philosophy, but rather through the physical practice of zazen. I think that, at least in the beginning, Zen attracted warriors of the period of feudal wars through its pragmatic aspect.

As I said earlier, a particular quality of budo is the fact that it takes pragmatism to the limit in such a way that it begins to become one with morality and philosophy. Analyzing the philosophy of budo only serves to accentuate the disparity between theory and practice, because intellectual comprehension creates the illusion of understanding something that in reality is built up out of experience.

The method of rentan, like that of Zen, seeks to arrive at the essence of budo without passing through the process of learning specific techniques. In the art of the sword, which demands the proper handling of the sword and correct sword strokes, this method is not applicable until after you have mastered a minimum of technique. For even if you have acquired mastery of your energy and developed an accurate perception of the action of combat, your movements will not translate into effective action if your sword does not follow the proper paths. By contrast, in the art of bare-handed combat, where it is a matter of delivering a blow and not of cutting with a blade, you can deliver an effective blow without the level of precision required by the sword. To the extent that you are able to produce sufficient impact, your blow can be effective without the same technical rigor that is required with the blade of a sword.

15

The Convergence of Two Approaches

Zen is inseparable from the practice of zazen, sitting meditation in the lotus posture. In the narrow sense of the term, the zazen posture is a kata with just one position. The beginner and the great master take the same posture. Seen from the outside, it is the same posture, but the content of it is different. The content is the physical sensation and the state of mind, that is, the ki. In effect, ki makes the difference between the beginner and the master.

In this connection, I would like to cite an example.

From the time of his adolescence, Harumitsa Hida (1883–1956) was looking for a method to strengthen his vital force. When he arrived at the formation of his own method, he thought that the state of his body and mind corresponded to the one sought in Zen. In an effort to verify this intuition, he had a number of encounters with practitioners and masters of Zen. He tells us:

One day, through the intercession of my friend, the monk Asaka, about twenty Zen monks came to see me. At their request, I gave some explanations about the relationship between the energy of the center and Zen. They were all moved by my talk. . . . In my turn, I asked them: "Would you be so kind as to show me your zazen." They immediately accepted my request and took the meditation posture for zazen. In observing them, I was surprised, because not one of them was sitting with a real center. . . . I told them: "With this way of doing zazen, you have neither a chest that is empty nor a head that is light. You are not able to enter into the state of emptiness and nonthought, am I right?" I asked each monk the same question. Every one of them answered me honestly, saying that he was not able to do so. I got the idea that to attain the state of a real center by means of Zen, it is necessary to practice wholeheartedly for twenty or thirty years.

Then I wanted to find out how a real master practices zazen. . . . I knew the name of the Zen master Iida from my older brother. I paid him a visit and asked him to instruct me in zazen. . . . He took the zazen posture, and I sat down facing him and watched him with the intention of penetrating to the very core of his mind. Lightly, the head and shoulders of the master straightened and raised until the instant when his center of gravity and the center of support of his body were superimposed. At that very instant, his body became immobile like a mountain. There was not the slightest defect in his posture. It was truly extraordinary! I was deeply moved to see before me the result of forty years of Zen. I paid homage by bowing my head low and said: "I have understood very well. I thank you. I would like to show you a few exercises from my method, which aims at strengthening the body." The master went to get his disciples, saying: "It would be a pity for me to watch by myself."

I sat down in my own way, and, at the instant when I struck my knees with my hands, he said: "This is similar to a sword that is capable of cutting without leaving its sheath; it catches on the sky and its blade is cold." Then I took my posture calmly, filling with force the sacred center and adopting a penetrating gaze. The master looked at me with great solemnity, leaning his body forward and several times uttering an exclamation. When I had finished, he told me: "This is a precise becoming-one with the way. The living way that will never die. It is not a method for attaining good health, because health is mortal, whereas your way is the eternal way. It is true Zen in movement, Zen through physical exercises. . . . It is absolutely necessary for you to transmit your method in written form. It is a treasure for humanity."

As this example reminds us, Zen, which directly aims for the essence and seeks the development of ki, is a practice— for the method of Zen, posture is absolutely primordial. Usually, the method of energy for arriving at ki is thought to be in opposition to the method of kata. Nevertheless, taking a precise posture with the sensation of a center is a form of kata in the rigorous sense of the term. In reality, working to- ward this well-defined posture is a means of arriving at the objective formulated by the way; and in the practice of this single posture there are a number of stages in which posture and mental representations condense into one.

The method of practice of yi quan is based mainly on the exercise of standing meditation (ritsu zen or zhang zhuang). This method is usually classified as in opposition to the method of kata, understood as a system of sequences of standardized movements. Nevertheless, we have seen that a kata does not necessarily have to include a movement; it could consist of one stationary posture. That is why I can make the statement that all the energy-oriented methods for arriving at and strengthening ki take the form of practice with kata.

There are a variety of religious methods for strengthening ki in the Japanese tradition. I will call attention to one of them, *sennichi kaiho gyu,* "the journey of a thousand days." This method is structured into several stages that take three years to complete. The last stage consists of walking a fixed mountain itinerary for one hundred consecutive days, stopping for prayers, taking very little nourishment. This extremely ascetic method takes practitioners to the very limits of their physical being. From the point of view of ki, I would analyze it as follows. By means of a very extreme and repetitious experience, the effects of which become stabilized over time, practitioners arrive at a kind of reorganization of their physical perceptions and their way of integrating them. As a monk who went through this experience said, "Because I ate so little, my mind and my body became so light they harmonized with the universe." This sentence bears witness to a transformation of his perceptive sensibility and to his opening to a dimension of awareness that corresponds to what is called ki in Japanese, a dimension of perception that is usually masked by the contingencies of our social life.

In these methods, which seek a form of religious illumination, I would call attention to the way in which ki is developed by means of standardized physical practices. This suggests an examination of the psychological structure that underlies these methods and of the points where that might also be present in the traditional practice of the martial arts. I find such a point of convergence in the structure of kata, whose mode of actualization I have analyzed through the martial arts.

16

Kiko and Combat

There exist a great number of schools of kiko, a method of strengthening qi or ki. Kiko is practiced with various goals in mind—in the struggle with illness, in an attempt to improve or fortify one's health, in the quest for well-being, and in the augmentation of physical capacities in the martial arts. All in all, the motivation for the practice of kiko is generally to improve one's physical condition. Nevertheless, if you go into this practice in depth, you will inevitably be led, if only a little, toward some sort of intuition of a dimension that engages your whole way of living.

For example, one of the keys to the practice in all schools of kiko is the breath. In kiko, breathing is not a simple mechanical movement. You associate it with various images as well as particular localized sensations.

When you breathe, if you have a negative thought (disgust, hatred, fear, malaise, and so on), your exercise will not succeed and could even have a negative effect. It is necessary for you to empty yourself of all negative thoughts and images. You should form some image of peace, tranquillity, or happiness and breathe with these positive images and with positive feelings. You can smile, but it should not be a forced smile; you can have a feeling of generosity, but it should not be generosity that is imposed or dictated by some belief—it has to be spontaneous.

Just as naturally as you seek out food that is appealing and good for your health, kiko leads you, outside of any moral considerations, to seek out positive thoughts and feelings. The fact is that whatever passes through your mind as you are breathing is absorbed deeply into your body, and it is also imprinted somewhere in your brain. As with food, it is in your interest to absorb elements that are positive for your being.

Thus you move in the direction of becoming detached from various elements of stress, because the more deeply and intensely you breathe, the more you sense that you are sending these elements into the depths of your body and diffusing them there. At that point you have the physical feeling of needing to get rid of these stressful elements.

The first thing the practice of kiko teaches you is to form positive images for the exercises, images that are inseparable from positive thoughts that make themselves felt as bodily sensations. This permits you to contact something essential that carries your vital flow.

In this way, kiko sharpens your senses by exploring your vision of your body as felt from the inside. At the same time, the more your body becomes permeable to the sensation of that which imparts life to it, the more the sharpness of its perception opens toward the outside, where it is taken up and extended by an immensity without limit.

We should note the following. In the course of their quest for well-being, adepts have clearly observed the direct links between thoughts and feelings and positive and negative images and their physical reactions. In the domain of the martial arts, we are aware that negative elements are also a source of effective action. Thus techniques exist in which you form an image of great sadness in order to produce a "cold" force, an image of great anger in order to produce a "black" force, and so on. The application of kiko to the martial arts is not always connected with the search for well-being. As a matter of personal choice, I shall leave this particular subject aside.

Making use of a number of exercises—I have drawn attention to only a few of them—kiko seeks to regulate the circulation of internal energy in the body, following the meridians long known to Chinese medicine. One of the main stages is the *shoshuten*, or stage of the "small circuit." There are a number of methods for practicing this.

"He who masters shoshuten will never know sickness." This aphorism from a Chinese classic has been cited many times. In classical Chinese practice, the pathway and the direction of the shoshuten are indicated: go downward following the center line of the body in the front, from the top of the head to the base of the abdomen; then go back up along the spinal column from the coccyx to the very top of the head. In the classical texts, only one direction is indicated. However, according to a recent discovery, the direction indicated in the classics indicates the direction of the current of the shoshuten for men; for women, the direction is the opposite, with a small percentage of exceptions.

During the process of working with this, trying to feel or orient the circulation of the energy in the opposite direction is difficult and creates a feeling of uneasiness. By contrast, once you have succeeded in establishing your sensation of the shoshuten firmly, you can exercise in the opposite direction without any sense of upset. By performing the exercise in the opposite direction from time to time, you can raise your level of shoshuten.

When you engage in combat with the orientation I have developed, you first try to upset your opponent's ki. Recently in my experiences of combat, I have become aware that disturbing my opponent's ki amounts to disturbing or blocking the flow of his shoshuten while at the same time maintaining the balance of my own shoshuten flow.

Those who have suffered this kind of disturbance in combat can analyze it if they are sufficiently advanced in kiko. This experience will permit them to orient their shoshuten exercises in such a way as to strengthen their shoshuten. Such an experience can become part of the process of strengthening ki through the practice of combat from the moment you have acquired an awareness of ki. If you lose a match because you have had your ki disturbed, you can strengthen your ki by directing your awareness introspectively to the state of your ki at the moment you lost. If you win a match, you can also reinforce your ki, because of your awareness of how you were able to maintain the stability of your ki in the dynamic situation of combat.

In sum, by seeking to develop sensitivity to ki, we can improve our efficiency in combat and find in combat another meaning beyond the mere attempt to win. We spontaneously become open to an ethical dimension. As far as I am concerned, it is through discovering this dimension that the martial arts acquire their full meaning for me, a meaning that fits well with our moment in history.

Conclusion

C ombat requires practice. It is possible to teach the theory or meaning of the martial arts on the basis of intellectual reflection, but if sufficient experience is lacking, your words will not have density and weight, even if they are correct. On the other hand, too often in martial arts circles, practice seems to become an end in itself, and the most important aspects of the disciplines, rich with potential, remain unformulated or are simply ignored.

My point of departure is Japanese budo. It seems to me to contain elements that allow it to go beyond cultural barriers and confer meaning on the contemporary practice of the arts of combat. The need to develop a budo practice of high quality is not only a Japanese problem. I have tried to bring out into the open cultural elements that are so obvious to the Japanese that they rarely rise to the surface of consciousness. This process has been possible for me only thanks to the clarity of Western culture. Through a two-way investigation, I have been able to better understand the functions of ki in the combat of budo and its implications. I am convinced that budo can be suitably put forward as a physical and mental practice for the future that will fit well with the cultural trends that are appearing today on a global scale.

Of course, one must at the same time come to grips with the techniques of budo, which are an essential part of it. The key to budo is found in our bodies: it is ki, but not just ki in general. In the practice of budo, we deal with ki as modulated in relation to a technical form, without which budo could not exist. And to the extent that the technical modulation of ki can be transmitted, we can bring into existence a form of communication through the combat of budo, one that can continue to be developed and deepened in a culturally differentiated fashion. Physical education and athletic training have reached an impasse; they are in the midst of a crisis that takes various forms. In my opinion, an analysis of the many dimensions of budo opens up a realm of thought whose significance goes beyond the strict confines of the martial arts. As far as the Japanese are concerned, I think we ought to have the openness of mind that would allow us to understand that other systems of thought exist in other cultures. This is indispensable for communication, and, more profoundly, it would also be the means for realizing and bringing to fruition in Japan itself everything that budo can contribute to a society characterized by its modernity.

Putting the emphasis on working with ki not only makes it possible to concretize the practice of budo but also opens up the prospect of long-term practice. In this way, budo can contribute to well-being and the strengthening of vital force. According to my analysis, the sensation of ki is the foundation of budo. This sensation can be felt regardless of cultural barriers. This opens up perspectives on the accessibility of budo to cultures completely outside the Buddhist and Shinto culture of Japan while at the same time preserving its specific quality.

In order to correct my posture, I look at myself in a mirror. Combat is like a mirror that reflects me to myself. Looking into this mirror, I become conscious of faults and inadequacies that have to be corrected and remedied. Therefore, in order to keep my life straight, I have to look in this mirror often. I would say that the practice of combat is a kind of ascetic practice for finding out who I am.

We are not talking simply about a way of winning in combat. The most important thing is the manner in which I conduct that combat, the quality of combat that I am able to realize. The combat of blows is determined by striking, but before striking the opponent, it is necessary for me to create the preliminary conditions, that is, to bring out the vulnerability in my opponent through the art of cadence, through changes in the distance between us, and through the projection of ki.

Nonetheless, when the moment of combat comes, I place my confidence in my instinct and my spontaneous energy. At that moment, I am neither scientific nor objective but profoundly subjective, and I let myself be guided by my subjective perception. Otherwise, I cannot carry on combat. Of course there are moments of speculation and objective observation, because the period of combat can be long or short. In any case, my perception is different from the perception with which I analyze and write according to ordinary logic. Combat permits me to verify in terms of concrete action whether my subjective sensation was accurate. If I am mistaken, the penalty is immediate, because I receive a blow. I cannot cheat.

When I speak of the quality of combat, I mean that you must conduct combat with this heightened perception. When you have the impression of sensing the opponent's field of ki and that you are succeeding in repulsing it or over-coming it with your own ki, you can create a postural and perceptive fault in your opponent and you will find the sure moment for a successful attack. That moment is the one dur-ing which the opponent is vulnerable, while you remain in a state of fullness. Your attack will inevitably succeed. A blow struck after you have created such a situation—that is, after you have won on a virtual level—is what is called an ippon. The ippon is therefore a movement of attack that confirms your virtual creation of the victory. In some way, it is a dou-bling of the victory, which makes it undeniable. This term is employed inappropriately in combat sports, because the ippon does not reside in a quality of technical movement, even if it is very spectacular.

As you have more and more combat experiences of trying to score ippon, you will begin to find out that if you let your-self be carried away by violence and aggression, you will lose your effectiveness. Doubtless violence can bring a first form of effectiveness, but with increasing age, you will begin to discover other sources of effectiveness. In any case, if you con-duct your combat at the age of sixty the way a youth of twenty does, you will not be very effective.

You will begin to perceive that if, feeling hatred and scorn, you want to hurt your opponent a lot, your opponent will feel your aggression, and the result will be that your at-tack risks being anticipated. And if you want to hurt the per-son facing you, perhaps there will be a voice inside your heart that whispers, "What you want to do is not good." For we are civilized beings who have received a moral education. This form of morality exists in all cultures, and it profoundly conditions our thinking and influences our actions—fortunately. As tiny as it might be, the inner voice might well hinder your action, and this can have important consequences in combat. In any case, if you continue to practice combat in seeking for the quality I have been speaking about, you will end up developing this kind of sensitivity. The effect will then be doubled, for emotion disturbs ki, and this takes its toll on your actions.

This sensitivity, then, forces you to introspection. You might think, "I wanted to strike, but my opponent knew it already by the time I made my attack. So my attack was predictable—something manifested despite my efforts to control it, something that warned my opponent of my action." Or else: "My action was hindered by a moment of hesitation, however slight, probably because something in me disapproved of the manifestation of my ego and my pride, which wanted to cause harm."

I do not know how this introspective process takes place for Westerners, but for the Japanese, such introspection is natural. It is in this sense that the tradition of the sword teaches us, "One's state of mind determines the quality of the sword." What is sought is a state of mind in which the act does not suffer the hindrance of ego, in which the expression of nonthought predominates. This leads us to a paradox: in order to carry on combat effectively, you must not think of harming your opponent; you must not think of winning.

Combat requires us to employ the resources we have developed through training at their maximum level, to bring our total capacity to the combat. For that, it is necessary to free ourselves from ineffectual thoughts, which are brakes on one's action. It is necessary to sharpen our perception to the point of being like the surface of calm water that clearly reflects the image of the moon. This effort coincides with the effort to transform one's mediocre ego into a better and superior self. The originally pragmatic idea of the art of combat—how to fight better, how to get better at dominating an opponent—takes on the additional, complementary objective of how to become better as a human being. And, with age, this complementary objective progressively becomes the practitioner's primary objective. This is the qualitative evolution that the martial arts have undergone over the course of history, and it is also the evolution followed by contemporary practitioners over the course of their practice. That is the meaning of budo.

What I have said might sound like just pretty words if you leave out the element of practice. It is not easy to approach combat in this manner, and often we try to identify only with the fruition and leave out the painful process of reaching it. This is just the same as the way that some intellectuals like to talk about Zen though they have practiced it little—they leave the long, hard journey out.

Martial arts circles bring together people of different inclinations. For some, violence is a kind of taboo, because the practice of violence is vulgar. Others plunge into it completely, and still others try to go beyond it. But going beyond violence is not easy. It is a problem. I do not believe that practicing just a little will be enough to enable one to go beyond violence. A number of forms of training too easily set aside the experience of combat. The reality of combat cannot be as spectacular and as infallible as martial arts demonstrations are. Combat is like a walk in the shadows, where one can never know everything in advance. There are always unknown elements.

Here I ask myself a personal question.

What is the point of becoming powerful in combat? What is the purpose of training in one or another method of combat?

I believe that if a martial art does nothing more than allow us to acquire skill in fighting, there is not much worth in it. To be able to fight a little bit better than others, what is the point of that?

I was initiated into the art of combat in my childhood, and up to this point I have practiced various forms of combat that are more or less violent. When I observe what happens in my mind and my body when I evoke these forms of combat mentally, I feel a certain malaise. This is due to aggression, to the uprush of violence, to the will to crush, in fact, kill the adversary, to the fear of receiving blows, to anticipation of the atmosphere of tension. . . . I have discovered that the cause of my malaise is rooted in the distortion, the compression of ki that I had to undergo over time without analyzing it and that the memory of my combats causes to well up. During a certain period in my youth, the tensions that arose from a confrontation permitted me to balance my own inner tension, and that made me feel a certain satisfaction and a certain pleasure; but nevertheless I always felt that this was not really what I should have done.

This form of satisfaction has nothing to do with what I caught sight of in the combat dimension of kendo, which goes beyond the animal confrontation of combat. Having acquired a level of accomplishment in kendo, I tried to integrate this dimension into my art of combat of punching and kicking. This was a spontaneous reaction on my part, because I had always questioned myself about the meaning of what I was doing, and as I continued in my practice, I had never encountered a satisfactory method. I was looking for something more in the art of combat than simple effectiveness and force. Whatever one's level of performance, a person's effectiveness in bare-handed combat, in the face of modern forms of combat, is very fragile and ephemeral. The goal of becoming strong and developing effectiveness in combat was not enough to make me persevere in the martial arts. I met many masters of great worth, and I received precious teachings. Nevertheless, no discipline, no method was satisfying to me, because I was searching for a martial art that corresponded fully on the physical and spiritual planes to the current conditions of life.

Looking for the meaning of the practice of combat, I ran into a wall, because the method and the manner of practicing combat had to conform to my philosophy and my intuition of life. It was only after forty years of practicing budo and twenty years of practicing kiko that I came to the concrete understanding that if I practiced budo with ki as my guide, my practice could find its full meaning, which is what I was looking for from the beginning.

I have given my school the name Jisei Budo. *Ji* means "oneself"; *sei* means "to form," or "to accomplish." Thus it is a school of budo through which one can form oneself by oneself. Each moment is therefore only a stage. The meaning of the practice of budo that I was looking for from the beginning was to forge my existence by my own means. Based on what I have learned, I have created a method of budo through which I try to train myself and forge myself. That is the meaning of Jisei and the direction I propose to my students.

Starting from that moment, ki opened to me a view of the world through physical sensation, and I have found myself engaged in a temporality that goes beyond me.

Starting with that moment, I arrived at a clear conception of combat. It is this. If you practice combat having developed sensitivity to ki and letting yourself be guided by ki, you can practice in an effective and meaningful fashion. At the same time, you will open your perception and sensitivity to whatever is taking place within you. You will then feel, in a concrete way, that you are attuned to the ki of all that surrounds you. This will make you feel what is negative about hatred; it will teach you to overcome fear and not to let yourself be hobbled by desire. In this sense, we can say that ki contains within it a morality, but this morality is situated beyond social and religious morality—it has its roots in your own experience.

Starting from there, the quest for effectiveness in combat also takes on the sense of internalizing an ethic.